Betty Crocker's

creative

Cookies

Macmillan • USA

MACMILLAN
A Simon & Schuster Macmillan Company
1633 Broadway
New York, NY 10019

MACMILLAN is a registered trademark of Macmillan, Inc.

BETTY CROCKER is a registered trademark of General Mills, Inc.

Library of Congress Cataloging-in-Publication Data

Crocker, Betty
   [Creative cookies]
   Betty Crocker's creative cookies.
         p.   cm.
   Includes index.
   ISBN 0-02-860366-4
     1. Cookies.   I. Title.   II. Title: Creative cookies.
TX772.C76   1995   95-4981
641.8'654—dc20   CIP

For consistent baking results, the Betty Crocker Food and Publications Center recommends Gold Medal flour

Front Cover (left to right): Cream Cheese Cookie Tarts (page 78), The Ultimate Valentine's Day Cookies (page 61), Frosted Chocolate Drop Cookies (page 23), Sugar Cookies (page 25), Mint Brownies (page 94) Chocolate-Wintergreen Refrigerator Cookies (page 38), Chocolate Bonbon Cookies (page 49), Nutty Marshmallow Bars (page 79), Sugar Cookie Cutouts (page 25), Granola Hermits (page 22)

Back Cover (top to bottom): Mint Brownies (page 94), Valentine's Day Cookies (page 61), Sugar Cookie Cutouts (page 25), Nutty Marshmallow Bars (page 79), Granola Hermits (page 22)
Title and Contents page: Sugar Cookie Tarts (page 26)

Manufactured in the United States of America
10 9 8 7 6 5 4 3 2 1

Contents

Introduction

The word cookie comes from the Dutch *keokje* meaning "little cake." Cookies have been a favorite American treat since the first colonists landed and our love for cookies has grown ever since. We are always dreaming up ways to improve or change them, dress them up or down, make them crispier or chewier, more simple or extravagant. From simple drop cookies, to easy refrigerator cookies, to hearty bars, cookies are still one of the best treats we can imagine, no matter what the occasion. And, what is more enticing than the aroma of cookies baking? We've collected some of the most appealing—and easy to prepare—cookie ideas here that are sure to inspire you whether you're selling them at a bake sale or just filling the jar at home.

What brings a smile to faces faster than the anticipation of biting into a freshly baked cookie? Whether it is a great classic such as the Ultimate Chocolate Chip Cookie or cookies that have a little bit of everything in them such as Peanut Butter Chip-Oatmeal Cookies, we have recipes to please everyone! Looking for recipes to impress? Try French Lace Cookies, Cocoa Mini Meringues or Hazelnut Sablé. If you have kids at home or you're a kid at heart, we've included an entire chapter filled with fun, from Thumbprint Cookies to a creative Cookie Pizza. Hungry for a hearty bar cookie? Lemon Squares, Toffee Bars and a wide range of brownies are sure to satisfy. And who could forget the holidays? We've got you covered from Valentine's Day to Christmas and Hanukkah, so you can make cookies for all occasions.

Homemade cookies are so many things, instant comfort, great afternoon snacks, easy desserts, picnic treats or whatever you'd like them to be. There is something special about cookies and you simply cannot have too many in the house. We've also included everything you'll need to know, from start to storage, with lots of baking tips and ideas for every cookie instance. We're sure you'll find *Betty Crocker's Creative Cookies* makes baking cookies a real treat!

Betty Crocker

Stocking the Cookie Jar

Before you roll up your sleeves and start mixing cookie dough, read the recipe through carefully. Nothing is more irritating than discovering that you need to make another trip to the store to fetch a critical ingredient. Be sure to assemble the equipment you need before you start. You probably have most of the necessary utensils (baking cookies calls for nothing very sophisticated in the way of equipment), but it is reassuring to know you have everything conveniently at hand.

Success Guidelines

The key to successful baking is adhering to a number of guidelines:

- Follow the recipe exactly, measuring the ingredients accurately.
- To ensure uniform baking, make all the cookies in one batch the same size.
- Follow directions for greasing (or greasing and flouring) baking sheets and pans.
- Allow the oven to heat to the temperature called for in the recipe.
- Use shiny cookie sheets rather than black steel ones. The black steel sheets speed browning on the bottom surface but frequently overbrown the bottom of cookies and leave the rest underdone.
- Bake one sheet of cookies at a time and position it on the center oven rack. Use a cookie sheet two inches shorter and narrower than the interior of your oven, so that hot air can circulate for even baking. If you must use two sheets, space them so that one is not directly over the other and switch the positions of the sheets halfway through the baking time.

About Ingredients

Flour: Use either bleached or unbleached all-purpose flour. Some recipes in which whole wheat flour can be substituted with success are indicated. Drop cookies made with stone-ground flour may spread more and have a coarser texture than those made with regular whole wheat flour.

Rolled Oats: Use either quick-cooking or old-fashioned rolled oats unless specified in recipe. Old-fashioned rolled oats make a chewier, slightly drier cookie. Quick-cooking oats are best for nonbaked recipes because they absorb moisture better and are less chewy.

Sugar: Sugar adds sweetness and color (by browning) and contributes to spreading. The higher the sugar-to-flour ratio in a recipe, the more tender and crisp the cookies will be.

Fat: Fats add tenderness and flavor to cookies. Butter and margarine both produce a crisper cookie than shortening and can be used interchangeably. Use stick butter or margarine rather than tub or whipped, which contain more added water. When recipes call for shortening, use the solid type made from hydrogenated vegetable oil. Shortening gives cookies a softer texture than margarine or butter, and the cookies can be somewhat drier and crumbly. Never substitute vegetable oil for a solid fat.

Cocoa: When recipes call for cocoa, use the unsweetened kind; do not use instant cocoa mix.

Chocolate: To melt chocolate, break it into small pieces (if it is not in pieces already). Place in a heatproof bowl or in the top of a double boiler set over very hot—not boiling—water. Stir occasionally while the chocolate melts. The microwave oven is a wonderful tool for melting chocolate, too. Stir at the minimum melting time; remember that chocolate can keep its shape even when it is almost melted. We use the following chocolate when baking cookies:

> **Semisweet Chocolate Chips:** These chocolate chips are sold in bags of 6 and 12 ounces.

> **Sweet Cooking Chocolate:** This is often labeled "sweet baking chocolate" and packaged in 4- or 8-ounce bars.

> **Unsweetened Chocolate:** Do not confuse "dark" or "bitter" chocolate with unsweetened chocolate; they contain considerable amounts of sugar. Unsweetened chocolate is conveniently available in paper-wrapped, 1-ounce squares.

Leavening: Virtually all baking powder on the market today is double-acting. This means it begins acting when mixed with a liquid and is activated a second time when heated in the oven. Baking soda will react only with an acid such as buttermilk, lemon juice or molasses. If leavening is old or has been exposed to moisture, cookies made with it will be dense and flat.

Eggs: Eggs add richness, moisture and structure to cookies. Too many eggs can make cookies crumbly. All of the recipes in this book have been tested with large eggs.

Liquids: Liquids tend to make cookies crisper by making them spread more.

Coconut: Sweetened coconut is best when packaged in airtight bags and cans. Whether you buy coconut flaked (small bits) or shredded (thicker, longer strands), it should be moist.

Corn Syrup: Corn syrup makes for somewhat elastic, easy-to-handle doughs. "Light" corn syrup is specified in recipes where the deeper flavor of "dark" corn syrup would be overbearing. If neither "light" nor "dark" is specified, either one may be used.

Nuts: When nuts are called for, you may use any sort of nuts you like. A number of cookies are made with blanched (skinned) almonds. You can buy blanched almonds or, if you don't mind the extra effort you can blanch whole almonds yourself. Simply cover the almonds with boiling water and let sit for 10 minutes. The skins should slip off easily. Nuts keep well in airtight packages, especially when refrigerated. But they don't keep indefinitely, so taste nuts before you add them to the dough; you don't want a rancid nut in your cookie.

Equipment to Have on Hand

Measuring spoons, graduated measuring cups, liquid measuring cups, mixing bowls, a wooden spoon, a rubber scraper, flatware teaspoons and tablespoons, a hand beater or electric mixer, three or four cookie sheets, a timer, a wide spatula (to remove cookies to cooling racks) and cooling racks are just some of the equipment to have on hand.

Use cookie sheets at least two inches narrower and shorter than oven so heat will circulate around them. Shiny, bright sheets are best for delicate browning. Watch cookies carefully if using a sheet with a nonstick coating—cookies may brown quickly; follow manufacturers' directions as many suggest reducing the oven temperature by 25°.

Measure Correctly

Graduated measuring spoons: Pour or scoop dry ingredients into spoon until full, then level off. Pour liquid into spoon until full.

Graduated measuring cups: Spoon flour or powdered sugar into cup, then level off with metal spatula or straight-edged knife. Do not tap cup or pack more into cup before leveling. Do not sift flour before measuring. Sift powdered sugar after measuring, if lumpy. Scoop granulated sugar into cup, then level off. To measure nuts, coconut and cut-up or small fruit, spoon into cup and pack down lightly. To measure brown sugar or shortening, spoon into cup and pack down firmly.

Liquid measuring cups: Pour in liquid to required level. Read the measurement at eye level.

Mixing

Use electric mixer when specified (speed and mixing times are given). Usually the sugars, fats and liquids are mixed together first, either by electric mixer according to directions, or by hand until ingredients are well combined. Then the dry ingredients are stirred in just until moistened. Air incorporated into the fat acts like a leavening. Cookies mixed by hand will be more compact and dense than cookies mixed with a mixer because there is less air beaten into the fat. Do not overmix or cookies will be tough.

Shaping

Drop Cookies: Spoon dough with a flatware spoon (not a measuring spoon) unless a level teaspoon or tablespoon is specified. If cookies spread too much, chill dough before dropping onto sheet. (Incorrect oven temperature and warm cookie sheet can also cause spreading.)

Rolled cookies: Many recipes call for rolling dough on a floured surface to prevent sticking. If recipe calls for using pastry cloth and cloth-covered rolling pin, rub flour into cloths before rolling. Roll lightly and evenly. When dough requires chilling, roll only part of the dough at a time and keep the remainder refrigerated. Dip cutters in flour and shake off excess before cutting. Cut cookies close together to avoid rerolling (rerolled dough will be a little tougher). Lift cookies to cookie sheet with spatula to avoid stretching.

Molded cookies: Take the time to make the cookies uniform so they will not only look nice but bake evenly. If dough is too soft to work with, cover and refrigerate about one hour or until firm. Chill wrapped rolls of refrigerator cookie dough until firm enough to slice easily with a sharp knife. Cut into thickness specified in recipe. If cut too thin, the cookies will be hard; if too thick, they will be soft.

Pressed cookies: Do not refrigerate dough for pressed cookies (unless specified in recipe) or they will be too stiff to push through the press. Test the dough for consistency before adding all the flour. The dough should be soft and pliable but not crumbly. If dough is too stiff, add one egg yolk. If too soft, add flour one tablespoon at a time until the correct consistency is achieved. There are several types of cookie presses on the market today. For best results, follow manufacturers' directions.

Bar cookies: Spread or press dough evenly to sides of pan. Use correct pan size; bars baked in a pan that is too large can become hard from overbaking and if baked in a pan too small, they may be doughy in center from underbaking. Cool bars in pan before cutting to prevent crumbling, unless recipe specifies cutting while warm.

Baking

Place cookie dough on greased or ungreased cookie sheet as directed. Bake a "test" cookie. If it spreads more than desired, add one to two tablespoons flour to the dough. If it is too dry, add one to two tablespoons milk. Always place dough on a cool cookie sheet—it will spread too much if placed on a hot one. Make all cookies on each cookie sheet one at a time, using middle rack. (If you wish to bake two sheets at once, remember to switch sheets halfway through baking.) Check at the minimum bake time. Watch cookies carefully while baking, as even one minute can make a difference. Cookies become crisper or harder the longer they are baked.

Doneness

Although bake times are stated in every recipe, a doneness test is also given. Sometimes the color of the cookie may be the best test (until light brown, or until edges begin to brown, for example). Sometimes, especially if the dough is dark, a color change is hard to see. Then, test might be until almost no indentation remains when touched in center. After baking one or two sheets you should get a feel for an approximate bake time. Use that time as your first check, but always use the doneness test as your final check.

Cooling

Some cookies need to be removed from the cookie sheet immediately after baking to prevent sticking. Some need to cool slightly (one to two minutes before removing to allow them time to set; otherwise, they will fall apart. The larger the cookie, the longer the cooking time, Follow recipes carefully. Always cool cookies on wire cooling racks to allow the air to flow all around the cookie to prevent sogginess. Cool cookies completely before frosting unless instructed to frost warm.

Storing

Store unbaked cookie dough tightly covered in the refrigerator for up to twenty-four hours. To store refrigerator cookie dough in the freezer, wrap shaped dough in vaporproof freezer wrap (waxed plastic wrap or aluminum foil). Label and freeze for up to six months. When ready to bake, slice frozen dough with a sharp knife.

Store crisp cookies in a loosely covered container. This allows the flow of air to keep them crisp. If they soften, heat in a 300° oven three to five minutes to recrisp. Store soft cookies in a tightly covered container to prevent moisture loss. A piece of bread or apple (replace frequently) in the container helps to keep the cookies soft.

Frosted cookies can be frozen for up to three months. Freeze them uncovered until they are firm, then pack in single layer in a container lined with freezer wrap with wrap between each layer. Seal the lining, close container, label and freeze. Let frozen cookies stand uncovered on serving plate about twenty minutes before serving.

Creative Decorating Ideas

Some plain cookies look their best that way. More often than not, though, cookies lend themselves to decoration. Sometimes decorating is answered by the amount of time you have but it doesn't have to be a time-consuming project. Decorating can takes less time than one might think.

The fun of decorating is letting your imagination roam. Many of the cookies in this book are accompanied by frosting or icing suggestions. The possibilities that go on are endless.

Here are just a few of those possibilities:

- Sprinkle frosted or iced cookies with chopped nuts. Press the nuts into the topping while it is still wet: that way, the nuts will hold fast to the cookie.

- Arrange raisins, currants or candied cherry halves or cherry cut-outs on pale-frosted cookies before the frosting or icing sets.

- Drizzle melted chocolate in abstract patterns over the tops of cookies. This is a great, easy way to dress up frosted or iced bar cookies.

- Dark-colored or chocolate-frosted cookies benefit from drizzled glazes, too. You can use any of the thinner powdered sugar glazes and even tint the glazes with food coloring if you like.

- A sprinkling of sifted, powdered sugar is enough to "dress" a plain cookie, whether dark or light. For large plain cookies that aren't very pale, center a paper doily over the cookie before sifting the sugar; then carefully remove the doily, leaving the sugar design.

- A decorating bag and assorted decorating tips make cookie decorating a snap. A good substitute, however, is a plastic freezer bag with 1/8 inch of one bottom corner snipped off to make a writing tip. Use Decorator's Frosting recipe (p.10) for spreading or piping.

- Rolled cookie dough is probably the most versatile dough for making special-occasion cookies. It can be cut into any shape and decorated before or after baking. Use the Egg Yolk Paint or Cookie Paint (p. 10) to paint light-colored, unbaked dough.

DECORATOR'S FROSTING

Makes enough to frost 3 to 5 dozen cookies.

Beat 2 cups powdered sugar, 1/2 teaspoon vanilla, and about 2 tablespoons half-and-half or milk until smooth and of spreading consistency. Frosting can be tinted with food color.

COOKIE PAINT

Tint small amounts of evaporated milk with different colors. Paint on cookie dough before baking.

EGG YOLK PAINT

Blend 1 egg yolk and 1/4 teaspoon water. Divide mixture among several custard cups. Tint with food colors to desired brightness. Paint on cookie dough before baking. If paint thickens on standing, add a few drops of water.

Special-Occasion Cutouts

Place Cards: Roll dough 1/4 inch thick. Cut into rectangles, 2 1/4 × 1 1/2 inches. Cut triangles from dough to make stands, slightly shorter than height of place cards and tapered to form an angle less than 90°. Bake as directed in recipe. Attach triangle to back of place card with frosting.

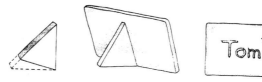

Cut triangles from dough to stand. Attach triangles to back of place cards with frosting. Decorate as desired.

Gift tags: Roll dough 1/8 to 3/16 inch thick. Cut into tag shapes, about 2 × 1 inch. Make holes with straw for string or ribbon to thread through. Bake as directed in recipe. Attach cooked cookies to packages just before giving them to recipients.

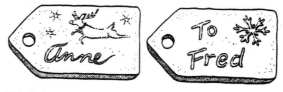

Make holes with straw before baking. Decorate as desired.

How to Use Nutrition Information

Nutrition Information per serving for each recipe includes the amounts of calories, protein, carbohydrate, fat, cholesterol and sodium.

- If ingredient choices are given, the first listed ingredient is used in recipe nutrition information calculations.
- When ingredient ranges or more than one serving size is indicated, the first weight or serving is used to calculate nutrition information.
- "If desired" ingredients and recipe variations are not included in nutrition information calculations.

Creative Cookie
Combinations

Bake Sale
Lemon Squares p. 81
Snickerdoodles p. 77
Ultimate Brownies p. 89
Chocolate Crinkles p. 18
Peanut Butter Chip-Oatmeal
Cookies p. 18

Cookie Jar Favorites
Chocolate Chip Cookies p. 14
Oaties p. 17
Peanut Butter Cookies p. 36
Hermits p. 22
Gingersnaps p. 36

Holiday Fun
Candy Cane Cookies p. 54
Christmas Bells p. 56
Cherry Blinks p. 57
Russian Teacakes p. 57
Almond-filled Crescents p. 59
Cappuccino-Pistachio Shortbread p. 28

Afternoon Tea
Butterscotch Shortbread p. 28
Peach Triangles p. 32
Hazelnut Sablés p. 43
Linzer Torte Bars p. 86
Lemon Tea Biscuits p. 48
Cream Wafers p. 46

College Care Package
Inside-out
Chocolate Chip Cookies p. 14
Scotch Shortbread p. 28
Banana-Oatmeal Drops p. 17
Peanut Butter-Chocolate Kisses p. 38
Marbled Brownies p. 89

Great Gift Ideas
Strawberry-Chocolate Cheesecake
Squares p. 85
Hungarian Poppy Seed Cookies p. 41
Raspberry Jam Strips p. 39
Chocolate Linzer Hearts p. 61
Truffle Cookies p. 51

Best Loved Birthday Treats
Animal Cookies p. 35
Cookie Pizza p. 69
Multigrain Cutouts p. 75
Cow Cookies p. 77
Peanut Butter Lollipop Cookies p. 70
Turtle Brownies p. 90

Triple-Chocolate Chunk Cookies

1

Drop Cookies

Triple-Chocolate Chunk Cookies

About 3 dozen cookies

A sweet trio of chocolates makes these cookies three times as delightful—creamy milk chocolate, more assertive bittersweet chocolate and soft white chocolate.

1 1/2 cups packed brown sugar
1 cup (2 sticks) margarine or butter, softened
1 egg
2 1/4 cups all-purpose flour
2 teaspoons ground cinnamon
1 teaspoon baking soda
1/2 teaspoon salt
1 cup chopped nuts
4 ounces bittersweet chocolate, chopped
4 ounces sweet cooking chocolate, chopped
4 ounces white chocolate (white baking bar), chopped
Three-Chocolate Glaze (right)

Heat oven to 375°. Mix brown sugar, margarine and egg. Stir in flour, cinnamon, baking soda and salt (dough will be soft). Stir in nuts, chocolates and white chocolate. Drop dough by rounded tablespoonfuls about 2 inches apart onto ungreased cookie sheet. Bake 8 to 10 minutes or until light golden brown. Cool slightly; remove from cookie sheet. Dip cookies in Three-Chocolate Glaze.

THREE-CHOCOLATE GLAZE

3 teaspoons shortening
3 ounces bittersweet chocolate
3 ounces sweet cooking chocolate
3 ounces white chocolate (white baking bar)

Heat 1 teaspoon shortening with bittersweet chocolate over low heat, stirring constantly, until chocolate is melted and smooth. Remove from heat. Dip each cookie 1/2-inch deep into chocolate along one edge. Repeat with remaining shortening and chocolates. Rotate dipped edge of cookie for each type of chocolate, if desired.

Serving Size: 1 Cookie Calories 220 (Calories from Fat 125); Fat 14 g (Saturated 5 g); Cholesterol 5 mg; Sodium 130 mg; Carbohydrate 24 g; (Dietary Fiber 2 g); Protein 2 g

The Ultimate Chocolate Chip Cookie

About 4 dozen cookies

3/4 cup granulated sugar
3/4 cup packed brown sugar
1 cup (2 sticks) margarine or butter, softened
1 egg
2 1/4 cups all-purpose flour
1 teaspoon baking soda
1/2 teaspoon salt
1 cup coarsely chopped nuts
2 cups (12 ounces) semisweet chocolate chips

Heat oven to 375°. Mix sugars, margarine and egg in large bowl. Stir in flour, baking soda and salt (dough will be stiff). Stir in nuts and chocolate chips.

Drop dough by rounded tablespoonfuls about 2 inches apart onto ungreased cookie sheet. Bake 8 to 10 minutes or until light brown (centers will be soft). Cool slightly; remove from cookie sheet. Cool on wire rack.

Serving Size: 1 Cookie Calories 135 (Calories from Fat 70); Fat 8 g (Saturated 2 g); Cholesterol 5 mg; Sodium 95 mg; Carbohydrate 16 g; (Dietary Fiber 1 g); Protein 1 g

Get the Scoop on Perfectly Shaped Drop Cookies

A trick to making drop cookies the same size is to use a spring-handle ice-cream scoop to drop the dough. Ice-cream scoops come in various sizes and are referred to by a number which corresponds to the number of level scoops per quart of ice cream. Use the size scoop that drops the amount of dough called for in your recipe. For example, if your recipe says to drop the dough by rounded teaspoonfuls, use a number 70 scoop.

Inside-out Chocolate Chip Cookies

About 4 1/2 dozen cookies

Creamy white chips in dark, chocolaty cookies—these chocolate chip cookies have been turned inside-out!

1 cup granulated sugar
3/4 cup packed brown sugar
3/4 cup (1 1/2 sticks) margarine or butter, softened
1/2 cup shortening
2 eggs
1 teaspoon vanilla
2 1/2 cups all-purpose flour
1/2 cup cocoa
1 teaspoon baking soda
1/4 teaspoon salt
1 1/2 cups vanilla milk chips
1 cup chopped nuts

Heat oven to 350°. Mix sugars, margarine, shortening, eggs and vanilla in large bowl. Stir in flour, cocoa, baking soda and salt. Stir in vanilla milk chips and nuts.

Drop dough by rounded tablespoonfuls about 2 inches apart onto ungreased cookie sheet. Bake 10 to 12 minutes or until set. Cool slightly; remove from cookie sheet.

Serving Size: 1 Cookie Calories 130 (Calories from Fat 70); Fat 8 g (Saturated 2 g); Cholesterol 10 mg; Sodium 65 mg; Carbohydrate 15 g; (Dietary Fiber 1 g); Protein 1 g

Inside-out Chocolate Chip Cookies

Two-Way Chocolate Cookies

3 to 4 dozen cookies

1 cup sugar
1/2 cup (1 stick) margarine or butter, softened
1/3 cup milk
4 ounces unsweetened chocolate, melted and cooled
1 egg
1 teaspoon vanilla
2 cups all-purpose flour
1/2 teaspoon baking powder
1/2 teaspoon salt
1 cup chopped pecans

Mix sugar, margarine, milk, chocolate, egg and vanilla in large mixer bowl. Beat in remaining ingredients on low speed, scraping bowl constantly, until soft dough forms. Use half the dough for Carmelitas and half for Coco-Nut Balls (right).

CARMELITAS

1/2 chocolate dough (above)
18 vanilla caramels or candied cherries, cut into halves
1 1/2 cups powdered sugar
1 ounce unsweetened chocolate, melted and cooled
2 tablespoons light corn syrup
2 to 3 tablespoons hot water

Cover and refrigerate dough at least 1 hour. Heat oven to 400°. Shape dough by rounded teaspoonfuls around caramel halves. Place on ungreased cookie sheet. Bake until set, about 7 minutes; cool. Beat remaining ingredients in small bowl until thickened. Swirl tops of cookies in chocolate mixture.

COCO-NUT BALLS

2 cups flaked coconut
1/2 chocolate dough (left)

Heat oven to 400°. Work the coconut into the chocolate dough. Shape dough by rounded teaspoonfuls into balls. Roll balls in additional coconut, if desired. Place on ungreased cookie sheet. Bake until set, about 7 minutes.

Serving Size: 1 Cookie Calories 180 (Calories from Fat 80); Fat 9 g (Saturated 4 g); Cholesterol 5 mg; Sodium 90 mg; Carbohydrate 24 g; (Dietary Fiber 1 g); Protein 2 g

Oatmeal Cookies

About 5 dozen cookies

1 1/4 cups sugar
1/2 cup (1 stick) margarine or butter, softened
1/3 cup molasses
2 eggs
2 cups quick-cooking oats
1 2/3 cups all-purpose flour
1 cup raisins, chopped nuts or flaked coconut
1 teaspoon baking soda
1 teaspoon ground cinnamon
1/4 teaspoon salt

Heat oven to 375°. Mix sugar, margarine, molasses and eggs. Stir in remaining ingredients. Drop dough by rounded teaspoonfuls about 2 inches apart onto ungreased cookie sheet. Bake 9 to 10 minutes or just until set. Cool slightly; remove from cookie sheet.

Serving Size: 1 Cookie Calories 70 (Calories from Fat 20); Fat 2 g (Saturated 1 g); Cholesterol 10 mg; Sodium 45 mg; Carbohydrate 12 g; (Dietary Fiber 0 g); Protein 1 g

Banana-Oatmeal Drops

About 4 dozen cookies

You'll go ape over these cookies. Try substituting chocolate chips in place of the nuts for an extra treat!

1 3/4 cups quick-cooking or regular oats
1 1/2 cups all-purpose flour
1 cup sugar
1 cup mashed bananas (2 to 3 medium)
3/4 cup shortening
1 egg
1 teaspoon salt
1 teaspoon ground cinnamon
1/2 teaspoon baking soda
1/4 teaspoon ground nutmeg
1/2 cup chopped nuts or raisins

Heat oven to 400°. Mix all ingredients. Drop by rounded teaspoonfuls about 2 inches apart onto ungreased cookie sheet. Bake until light brown, about 10 minutes.

Serving Size: 1 Cookie Calories 85 (Calories from Fat 35); Fat 4 g (Saturated 1 g); Cholesterol 5 mg; Sodium 60 mg; Carbohydrate 11 g; (Dietary Fiber 0 g); Protein 1 g

Oaties

About 3 dozen cookies

1 1/4 cups all-purpose flour
1 cup quick-cooking oats
1 teaspoon ground cinnamon
1/2 teaspoon baking soda
1/8 teaspoon salt
3 egg whites or 1/2 cup cholesterol-free egg product
1/2 cup packed brown sugar
1/4 cup granulated sugar
1/3 cup unsweetened applesauce
1/4 cup (1/2 stick) margarine or butter, softened
1 teaspoon vanilla
1 cup raisins or chopped dried fruit

Heat oven to 325°. Spray cookie sheet with non-stick cooking spray. Mix flour, oats, cinnamon, baking soda and salt; reserve. Beat egg whites in large bowl on medium speed until foamy. Add sugars, applesauce, margarine and vanilla. Beat on medium speed until smooth. Add flour mixture; beat on low speed just until mixed. Stir in raisins.

Drop dough by tablespoonfuls 2 inches apart onto cookie sheet; flatten slightly. Bake 12 to 15 minutes or until light brown. Cool slightly; remove from cookie sheet. Cool on wire rack.

Serving Size: 1 Cookie Calories 65 (Calories from Fat 10); Fat 1 g (Saturated 0 g); Cholesterol 0 mg; Sodium 45 mg; Carbohydrate 13 g; (Dietary Fiber 0 g); Protein 1 g

Double-Chocolate Oatmeal Cookies

About 5 1/2 dozen cookies

These sturdy cookies travel well in care packages.

1 1/2 cups sugar
1 cup (2 sticks) margarine or butter, softened
1 egg
1/4 cup water
1 teaspoon vanilla
1 1/4 cups all-purpose flour
1/3 cup cocoa
1/2 teaspoon baking soda
1/2 teaspoon salt
3 cups quick-cooking oats
1 cup (6 ounces) semisweet chocolate chips

Heat oven to 350°. Mix sugar, margarine, egg, water and vanilla. Stir in remaining ingredients. Drop dough by rounded teaspoonfuls about 2 inches apart onto ungreased cookie sheet. Bake until almost no indentation remains when touched, 10 to 12 minutes. Remove immediately from cookie sheet.

Serving Size: 1 Cookie Calories 85 (Calories from Fat 35); Fat 4 g (Saturated 1 g); Cholesterol 5 mg; Sodium 60 mg; Carbohydrate 11 g; (Dietary Fiber 0 g); Protein 1g

Peanut Butter Chip-Oatmeal Cookies

About 6 dozen cookies

1 1/2 cups packed brown sugar
1 cup (2 sticks) margarine or butter, softened
1/4 cup shortening
1 tablespoon milk
2 teaspoons vanilla
1 egg
2 cups all-purpose flour
1/2 teaspoon baking soda
1/2 teaspoon salt
1 1/2 cups quick-cooking oats
1/2 cup chopped walnuts
2 cups (12 ounces) peanut butter chips

Heat oven to 375°. Mix brown sugar, margarine, shortening, milk, vanilla and egg in large bowl. Stir in flour, baking soda and salt. Stir in remaining ingredients.

Drop dough by rounded teaspoonfuls about 2 inches apart onto ungreased cookie sheet. For soft cookies, bake 10 to 12 minutes or until light brown; for crisp cookies, bake 12 to 14 minutes. Store tightly covered.

Serving Size: 1 Cookie Calories 95(Calories from Fat 45); Fat 5 g (Saturated 2 g); Cholesterol 5 mg; Sodium 60 mg; Carbohydrate 11 g; (Dietary Fiber 0 g); Protein 1 g

Macaroons

About 3 dozen cookies

Usually, macaroons are made with either almonds or coconut. These chewy delights contain both, cooked together on top of the stove and then dropped into tiny mounds and baked. Store in an airtight container to keep them moist.

1 package (3 1/2 ounces) almond paste, cut up
1/2 cup sugar
3 egg whites
1 package (7 ounces) flaked coconut

Heat oven to 300°. Grease and flour cookie sheet or use parchment paper. Mix almond paste, sugar and egg whites in saucepan. Cook over medium heat 6 to 8 minutes, stirring vigorously, until path remains when spoon is drawn through mixture; remove from heat. Stir in coconut.

Drop mixture by rounded teaspoonfuls about 1 inch apart onto cookie sheet. Bake 25 to 30 minutes or until light brown. Cool slightly; remove from cookie sheet.

Serving Size: 1 Cookie Calories 60 (Calories from Fat 25); Fat 3 g (Saturated 2 g); Cholesterol 0 mg; Sodium 20 mg; Carbohydrate 7 g; (Dietary Fiber 0 g); Protein 1 g

Chocolate Crinkles

About 6 dozen cookies

1/2 cup vegetable oil
4 ounces unsweetened chocolate, melted and cooled
2 cups granulated sugar
2 teaspoons vanilla
4 eggs
2 cups all-purpose flour
2 teaspoons baking powder
1/2 teaspoon salt
1/2 cup powdered sugar

Mix oil, chocolate, granulated sugar and vanilla in large bowl. Stir in eggs, one at a time, until blended. Stir in flour, baking powder and salt. Cover and refrigerate about 3 hours or until chilled.

Heat oven to 350°. Grease cookie sheet. Shape dough by rounded teaspoonfuls into balls. Roll in powdered sugar. Place about 2 inches apart on cookie sheet. Bake 10 to 12 minutes. Remove from cookie sheet.

Serving Size: 1 Cookie Calories 70 (Calories from Fat 25); Fat 3 g (Saturated 1 g); Cholesterol 10 mg; Sodium 30 mg; Carbohydrate 10 g; (Dietary Fiber 0 g); Protein 1 g

Chocolate Crinkles

Lemon-Ginger Crinkles

About 4 dozen cookies

1 cup packed brown sugar
1/2 cup shortening
1 egg
1 tablespoon grated lemon peel
1 1/2 cups all-purpose flour
1/2 teaspoon baking soda
1/2 teaspoon cream of tartar
1/4 teaspoon salt
1/4 teaspoon ground ginger
Granulated sugar

Heat oven to 350°. Mix brown sugar, shortening, egg and lemon peel in large bowl. Stir in flour, baking soda, cream of tartar, salt and ginger.

Shape dough into 1-inch balls; dip tops into granulated sugar. Place balls, sugared sides up about 3 inches apart on ungreased cookie sheet. Bake 10 to 11 minutes or until almost no indentation remains when touched.

Serving Size: 1 Cookie Calories 60 (Calories from Fat 20); Fat 2 g (Saturated 0 g); Cholesterol 5 mg; Sodium 40 mg; Carbohydrate 10 g; (Dietary Fiber 0 g); Protein 0 g

Molasses Crinkles

About 3 dozen cookies

1 cup packed brown sugar
1/2 cup (1 stick) margarine or butter, softened
1/4 cup shortening
1/4 cup molasses
1 egg
2 cups all-purpose flour
2 teaspoons baking soda
1 teaspoon ground cinnamon
1 teaspoon ground ginger
1/2 teaspoon ground cloves
1/4 teaspoon salt
Granulated sugar

Mix brown sugar, margarine, shortening, molasses and egg in medium bowl. Stir in remaining ingredients except granulated sugar. Cover and refrigerate at least 1 hour, but no longer than 24 hours.

Heat oven to 375°. Shape dough into 1 1/4-inch balls; roll in granulated sugar. Place about 2 inches apart on ungreased cookie sheet. Bake 10 to 11 minutes or just until set. Cool slightly; remove from cookie sheet.

Serving Size: 1 Cookie Calories 100 (Calories from Fat 35); Fat 4 g (Saturated 1 g); Cholesterol 5 mg; Sodium 120 mg; Carbohydrate 15 g; (Dietary Fiber 0 g); Protein 1 g

Raisin-Spice Cookies

About 18 cookies

1 cup (2 sticks) margarine or butter, softened
1 cup packed brown sugar
3/4 cup granulated sugar
1 teaspoon vanilla
2 eggs
2 1/4 cups all-purpose flour
1 teaspoon ground cinnamon
3/4 teaspoon baking soda
1/2 teaspoon salt
1/2 teaspoon ground cloves
1 cup quick-cooking oats
1 cup raisins

Heat oven to 375°. Beat margarine and sugars in large bowl on medium speed 5 minutes or until fluffy. Beat in vanilla and eggs. Beat in flour, cinnamon, baking soda, salt and cloves on low speed. Stir in oats and raisins.

Drop dough by 1/4 cupfuls about 2 inches apart onto ungreased cookie sheet; flatten slightly with fork. Bake 11 to 14 minutes or until edges are light brown. Let stand 3 to 4 minutes before removing from cookie sheet. Cool on wire rack.

Serving Size: 1 Cookie Calories 275 (Calories from Fat 100); Fat 11 g (Saturated 2 g); Cholesterol 25 mg; Sodium 240 mg; Carbohydrate 42 g; (Dietary Fiber 1 g); Protein 3 g

Molasses Crinkles, Peanut Butter Cookies (p.36)

Hermits

About 7 1/2 dozen cookies

2 cups packed brown sugar
1/2 cup shortening
1/2 cup (1 stick) margarine or butter, softened
1/2 cup cold coffee
2 eggs
3 1/2 cups all-purpose flour
1 teaspoon baking soda
1 teaspoon ground nutmeg
1 teaspoon ground cinnamon
1/2 teaspoon salt
1 1/2 cup raisins
1 cup chopped nuts

Heat oven to 375°. Mix brown sugar, shortening, margarine, coffee and eggs in large bowl. Stir in flour, baking soda, nutmeg, cinnamon and salt. Stir in raisins and nuts. Drop dough by rounded teaspoonfuls about 2 inches apart onto ungreased cookie sheet. Bake 8 to 10 minutes or until almost no indentation remains when touched. Cool slightly; remove from cookie sheet.

Serving Size: 1 Cookie Calories 75 (Calories from Fat 25); Fat 3 g (Saturated 1 g); Cholesterol 5 mg; Sodium 35 mg; Carbohydrate 11 g; (Dietary Fiber 0 g); Protein 1 g

Granola Hermits

About 4 dozen cookies

1 cup packed brown sugar
1/4 cup (1/2 stick) margarine or butter, softened
1/4 cup shortening
1/4 cup cold coffee
1/2 teaspoon baking soda
1/2 teaspoon salt
1/2 teaspoon ground cinnamon
1/2 teaspoon ground nutmeg
1 egg
1 3/4 cups all-purpose flour
1 cup raisins
1 cup granola, slightly crushed
1 cup candy-coated chocolate candies

Heat oven to 375°. Mix brown sugar, margarine, shortening, coffee, baking soda, salt, cinnamon, nutmeg and egg in a large bowl. Stir in remaining ingredients.

Drop dough by rounded teaspoonfuls about 2 inches apart onto ungreased cookie sheet. Bake 8 to 10 minutes or until almost no indentation remains when touched. Immediately remove from cookie sheet.

Serving Size: 1 Cookie Calories 100 (Calories from Fat 35); Fat 4 g (Saturated 2 g); Cholesterol 5 mg; Sodium 55 mg; Carbohydrate 15 g; (Dietary Fiber 0 g); Protein 1 g

---

Move Over Chocolate Chips

Today instead of chocolate chips, you can stir many other exciting treats into cookies for a fun change of pace. Our creative Stir-in Morsels (listed below) are sure to please the cookie lovers in your house and bring new life to cookie enjoyment. Mix and match the plain or chocolate cookie recipes with any of our new cookie stir-ins for tummy-tickling results.

Candy
Chocolate mint waffers, chopped
Chocolate toffee crunch
  thin candies
Milk chocolate-covered raisins
Chocolate-covered peanuts,
  coarsely chopped
Candy coated chocolate chips

Nuts
Pistachio nuts, chopped
Macadamia nuts,
  coarsely chopped
Trail mix combinations
  (nuts and raisins)

Fruit
Maraschino cherries,
  chopped and well drained
Dried fruit bits
Dried cranberries

Colorful Sour Cream Cookies

About 6 dozen cookies

Try tinting the dough different colors to fit any occasion.

1 cup sugar
2/3 cup margarine or butter, softened
1 teaspoon vanilla
2 eggs
1/2 cup sour cream
2 3/4 cups all-purpose flour
1 teaspoon baking soda
1/2 teaspoon salt
1/2 teaspoon ground nutmeg
Few drops yellow and green food color
Raisins or nuts

Heat oven to 375°. Lightly grease cookie sheet. Mix sugar, margarine, vanilla and eggs in medium bowl. Stir in sour cream. Stir in flour, baking soda, salt and nutmeg. Divide dough in half. Tint 1 half with yellow food color and the other half with green food color.

Drop dough by heaping teaspoonfuls onto cookie sheet. Press raisin into center of each cookie. Bake 8 to 10 minutes or until light brown.

Serving Size: 1 Cookie Calories 50 (Calories from Fat 20); Fat 2 g (Saturated 1 g); Cholesterol 5 mg; Sodium 55 mg; Carbohydrate 7 g; (Dietary Fiber 0 g); Protein 1 g

Frosted Chocolate Drop Cookies

About 4 1/2 dozen cookies

1 cup sugar
1/2 cup (1 stick) margarine or butter, softened
1/3 cup buttermilk or water
1 teaspoon vanilla
1 egg
2 ounces unsweetened chocolate, melted and cooled
1 3/4 cups all-purpose flour
1/2 teaspoon baking soda
1/2 teaspoon salt
1 cup chopped nuts
Chocolate Frosting (below)

Heat oven to 400°. Mix sugar, margarine, buttermilk, vanilla, egg and chocolate in a large bowl. Stir in flour, baking soda and salt. Stir in nuts.

Drop dough by rounded teaspoonfuls about 2 inches apart onto ungreased cookie sheet. Bake 8 to 10 minutes or until almost no indentation remains when touched. Immediately remove from cookie sheet; cool. Frost with Chocolate Frosting.

CHOCOLATE FROSTING

2 ounces unsweetened chocolate
2 tablespoons margarine or butter
3 tablespoons water
About 2 cups powdered sugar

Heat chocolate and margarine over low heat until melted; remove from heat. Sir in water and powdered sugar until smooth and spreading consistency.

Serving Size: 1 Cookie Calories 95 (Calories from Fat 45); Fat 12 g (Saturated 1 g); Cholesterol 5 mg; Sodium 60 mg; Carbohydrate 12 g; (Dietary Fiber 0 g); Protein 1 g

Butterscotch Shortbread (p.28)

2

Rolled Cookies

Sugar Cookies

About 5 dozen cookies

We have provided you with two of the best sugar cookie recipes here. Try this one if you want a crispier cookie. If a tender, more cakelike cookie is what you're after, try Sugar Cookie Cutouts.

1 1/2 cups powdered sugar
1 cup (2 sticks) margarine or butter, softened
1 teaspoon vanilla
1/2 teaspoon almond extract
1 egg
2 1/2 cups all-purpose flour
1 teaspoon baking soda
1 teaspoon cream of tartar
Granulated sugar

Mix powdered sugar, margarine, vanilla, almond extract and egg in large bowl. Stir in remaining ingredients except granulated sugar. Cover and refrigerate at least 2 hours.

Heat oven to 375°. Grease cookie sheet lightly. Divide dough in half. Roll each half 1/4 inch thick on lightly floured surface. Cut into desired shapes with 2- to 2 1/2-inch cookie cutters. Sprinkle with granulated sugar. Place on cookie sheet. Bake 7 to 8 minutes or until edges are light brown; cool.

Serving Size: 1 Cookie Calories 65 (Calories from Fat 25); Fat 3 g (Saturated 1 g); Cholesterol 5 mg; Sodium 60 mg; Carbohydrate 9 g; (Dietary Fiber 0 g); Protein 1 g

Sugar Cookie Cutouts

About 4 1/2 dozen cookies

For added fun, these cookies are perfect for painting. Make Egg Yolk Paint (page 10), decorate and bake as directed.

1 cup sugar
1/4 cup (1/2 stick) butter or margarine, softened
1/4 cup shortening
1 teaspoon vanilla
1 egg
2 2/3 cups all-purpose flour
1/2 cup sour cream
1 teaspoon baking powder
1/2 teaspoon baking soda
1/2 teaspoon salt
1/4 teaspoon ground nutmeg

Heat oven to 425°. Mix 1 cup sugar, margarine, shortening, vanilla and egg in large bowl. Stir in remaining ingredients. Divide dough into 3 parts.

Roll each part 1/4 inch thick on lightly floured surface. Cut with 2-inch cookie cutter. Place on ungreased cookie sheet. Bake 6 to 8 minutes or until no indentation remains when touched. Remove from cookie sheet.

Serving Size: 1 Cookie Calories 60 (Calories from Fat 20); Fat 2 g (Saturated 1 g); Cholesterol 5 mg; Sodium 55 mg; Carbohydrate 9 g; (Dietary Fiber 0 g); Protein 1 g

Butterscotch Sugar Cookies

About 4 dozen cookies

1 cup packed brown sugar
1/2 cup (1 stick) margarine or butter, softened
1/4 cup shortening
1 teaspoon vanilla
2 eggs
2 1/2 cups all-purpose flour
1 teaspoon baking powder
1 teaspoon salt
1 cup chopped black walnuts, if desired

Mix brown sugar, margarine, shortening, vanilla and eggs in medium bowl. Blend in flour, baking powder and salt. Stir in walnuts. Cover and refrigerate at least 1 hour.

Heat oven to 400°. Roll dough 1/8 inch thick on lightly floured cloth-covered surface. Cut into desired shapes with 3-inch cookie cutters. Place on ungreased cookie sheet. Bake 6 to 8 minutes or until very light brown. Immediately remove from cookie sheet.

Serving Size: 1 Cookie Calories 70 (Calories from Fat 25); Fat 3 g (Saturated 2 g); Cholesterol 15 mg; Sodium 70 mg; Carbohydrate 10 g; (Dietary Fiber 0 g); Protein 1 g

---

Rolling Tips

To make delicious rolled cookies, follow these tips. Start with properly chilled dough. Avoid re-rolling the dough more than twice; aim to roll it out once then assemble any "scraps" and roll them out together (once, or at the most, twice). Dust the dough, rolling pin and work surface with just enough flour to keep the dough from sticking, because excess flour makes cookies tough. Dough that is very sticky can be rolled between sheets of waxed paper.

Sugar Cookie Tarts

About 2 1/2 dozen cookies

To prevent fresh fruit from browning, toss fruit in a little lemon juice before placing on tarts.

2 cups sugar
1 cup shortening
3/4 cup (1 1/2 sticks) margarine or butter, softened
2 teaspoons vanilla
1 egg
3 1/2 cups all-purpose flour
1 teaspoon baking powder
1/4 teaspoon salt
Cream Cheese Spread (below)
Toppings (sliced fresh fruit, miniature chocolate chips, chopped pecans or jam and toasted sliced almonds)

Heat oven to 375°. Mix sugar, shortening, margarine, vanilla and egg in large bowl. Stir in flour, baking powder and salt. Roll half of dough at a time 1/4 inch thick on lightly floured surface. Cut into 3-inch rounds. Place 2 inches apart on ungreased cookie sheet. Bake 10 to 12 minutes or until light brown. Cool slightly; remove from cookie sheet. Cool completely. Prepare Cream Cheese Spread. Spread about 2 teaspoons over each cookie. Arrange toppings on spread. Refrigerate any remaining cookies.

CREAM CHEESE SPREAD

1/2 cup sugar
1 teaspoon vanilla
1 package (8 ounces) cream cheese, softened

Mix ingredients until smooth.

Serving Size: 1 Cookie Calories 270 (Calories from Fat 145); Fat 16 g (Saturated 5 g); Cholesterol 15 mg; Sodium 115 mg; Carbohydrate 30 g; (Dietary Fiber 0 g); Protein 2 g

Sugar Cookie Tarts

Scotch Shortbread

About 2 dozen 1 1/2- x 1-inch cookies

3/4 cup (1 1/2 sticks) margarine or butter, softened
1/4 cup sugar
2 cups all-purpose flour

Heat oven to 350°. Mix margarine and sugar. Stir in flour. (If dough is crumbly, mix in 1 to 2 tablespoons margarine or butter, softened.) Roll dough 1/2 inch thick on lightly floured surface. Cut into small shapes about 1 1/2- × 1-inch (leaves, ovals, squares, triangles, etc.). Place 1/2 inch apart on ungreased cookie sheet. Bake about 20 minutes or until set; cool.

Serving Size: 1 Cookie Calories 100 (Calories from Fat 55); Fat 6 g (Saturated 1 g); Cholesterol 0 mg; Sodium 65 mg; Carbohydrate 10 g; (Dietary Fiber 0 g); Protein 1 g

Butterscotch Shortbread

About 4 dozen cookies

If you prefer shortbread cutouts, use a 2-inch cookie cutter.

1/2 cup (1 stick) margarine or butter, softened
1/2 cup shortening
1/2 cup packed brown sugar
1/4 cup granulated sugar
2 1/4 cups all-purpose flour
1 teaspoon salt

Heat oven to 300°. Mix margarine, shortening and sugars in large bowl. Stir in flour and salt. (Dough will be dry and crumbly. Use hands to mix completely.) Roll dough into rectangle, 15 × 7 1/2 inches, on lightly floured surface. Cut into 1 1/2-inch squares. Place about 1 inch apart on ungreased cookie sheet. Bake about 25 minutes or until set. (These cookies brown very little, and the shape does not change.) Remove from cookie sheet.

Serving Size: 1 Cookie Calories 70 (Calories from Fat 35); Fat 4 g (Saturated 1 g); Cholesterol 0 mg; Sodium 70 mg; Carbohydrate 8 g; (Dietary Fiber 0 g); Protein 1 g

Cappuccino-Pistachio Shortbread

32 cookies

1 envelope (0.77 ounce) cappuccino coffee mix (from 2.65-ounce package)
1 tablespoon water
3/4 cup (1 1/2 sticks) margarine or butter, softened
1/2 cup powdered sugar
2 cups all-purpose flour
1 cup chopped pistachio nuts
1 ounce semisweet chocolate
1 teaspoon shortening

Heat oven to 350°. Dissolve coffee in water in medium bowl. Stir in margarine and powdered sugar. Stir in flour and 1/2 cup of the nuts, using hands if necessary, until stiff dough forms.

Divide dough in half. Shape each half into a ball. Pat each ball into 6-inch round, about 1/2 inch thick, on lightly floured surface. Cut each round into 16 wedges. Arrange wedges on ungreased cookie sheet about 1/2 inch apart with pointed ends toward center.

Bake about 15 minutes or until golden brown. Immediately remove from cookie sheet. Cool completely on wire rack.

Place remaining 1/2 cup nuts in small dish. Place chocolate and shortening in small microwavable bowl. Microwave uncovered on Medium (50%) 3 to 4 minutes, stirring after 2 minutes, until mixture can be stirred smooth and is drizzling consistency. Dip 1 edge of each cookie into chocolate, then into nuts. Place on waxed paper until chocolate is firm.

Serving Size: 1 Cookie Calories 105 (Calories from Fat 65); Fat 7 g (Saturated 1 g); Cholesterol 0 mg; Sodium 55 mg; Carbohydrate 10 g; (Dietary Fiber 1 g); Protein 2 g

Malted Milk Cookies

About 5 dozen cookies

These delightful cookies have the great taste of a malted milk treat!

2 cups packed brown sugar
1 cup (2 sticks) margarine or butter, softened
1/3 cup sour cream
2 eggs
2 teaspoons vanilla
4 3/4 cups all-purpose flour
3/4 cup natural malted milk powder
2 teaspoons baking powder
1/2 teaspoon baking soda
1/2 teaspoon salt
Malted Milk Frosting (below)

Heat oven to 375°. Mix brown sugar, margarine, sour cream, eggs and vanilla in large bowl. Stir in flour, malted milk powder, baking powder, baking soda and salt.

Roll one-third of dough at a time 1/4 inch thick on floured surface. Cut into 2 1/2-inch rounds. Place about 2 inches apart on ungreased cookie sheet Bake 10 to 11 minutes or until almost no indentation remains when touched in center. Immediately remove from cookie sheet. Cool completely. Prepare Malted Milk Frosting and spread on cookies.

Malted Milk Frosting

1/2 cup packed brown sugar
1/4 cup (1/2 stick) margarine or butter
4 to 5 tablespoons milk or half-and-half
3 3/4 cups powdered sugar
1/3 cup natural malted milk powder
1/2 teaspoon vanilla

Heat brown sugar, margarine and milk in 2-quart saucepan over medium heat until margarine is melted; remove from heat. Stir in remaining ingredients until smooth.

Serving Size: 1 Cookie Calories 145 (Calories from Fat 35); Fat 4 g (Saturated 1 g); Cholesterol 10 mg; Sodium 100 mg; Carbohydrate 26 g; (Dietary Fiber 0 g); Protein 1 g

New Mexico Biscochitos

About 4 dozen 2-inch cookies

Biscochitos are Mexico's answer to the Old World seed cookie—and are as easy to roll out and cut as sugar cookies. Biscochitos are the official state cookie of New Mexico.

1 cup sugar
1 cup (2 sticks) margarine or butter, softened
3 tablespoons sweet sherry
1 egg
3 cups all-purpose flour
2 teaspoons baking powder
2 teaspoons anise seed, crushed
1/4 teaspoon salt
1/4 cup sugar
1 teaspoon ground cinnamon

Heat oven to 350°. Mix sugar, margarine, sherry and egg in large bowl. Stir in remaining ingredients except 1/4 cup sugar and the cinnamon. Divide dough into halves. Roll each half 1/4 inch thick on lightly floured board.

Cut into desired shapes with cookie cutters; place on ungreased cookie sheet. Mix 1/4 cup sugar and the cinnamon; sprinkle on cookies. Bake until light golden brown, 10 to 12 minutes.

Serving Size: 1 Cookie Calories 85 (Calories from Fat 35); Fat 4 g (Saturated 1 g); Cholesterol 5 mg; Sodium 80 mg; Carbohydrate 11 g; (Dietary Fiber 0 g); Protein 1 g

Moravian Ginger Cookies

*About 1 dozen 1/8-inch-thick cookies or
about 1 1/2 dozen paper-thin cookies*

1/3 cup molasses
1/4 cup shortening
2 tablespoons packed brown sugar
1 1/4 cups all-purpose or whole wheat flour
1/4 teaspoon salt
1/4 teaspoon baking soda
1/4 teaspoon baking powder
1/4 teaspoon ground cinnamon
1/4 teaspoon ground ginger
1/4 teaspoon ground cloves
Dash of ground nutmeg
Dash of ground allspice
Easy Creamy Frosting (below)

Mix molasses, shortening and brown sugar in large bowl. Stir in remaining ingredients except Easy Creamy Frosting. Cover and refrigerate about 4 hours or until firm.

Heat oven to 375°. Roll half of dough at a time 1/8 inch thick or paper-thin on floured, cloth-covered surface. Cut into 3-inch rounds with floured cutter. Place about 1/2 inch apart on ungreased cookie sheet. Bake 1/8-inch-thick cookies about 8 minutes; paper-thin cookies about 5 minutes or until light brown. Immediately remove from cookie sheet. Cool completely. Prepare Easy Creamy Frosting and spread on cookies.

EASY CREAMY FROSTING

1 cup powdered sugar
1 to 2 tablespoons half-and-half
1/2 teaspoon vanilla

Mix ingredients until of spreading consistency.

Serving Size: 1 Cookie Calories 165 (Calories from Fat 45); Fat 5 g (Saturated 1 g); Cholesterol 0 mg; Sodium 85 mg; Carbohydrate 29 g; (Dietary Fiber 0 g); Protein 1 g

Joe Froggers

About 3 dozen cookies

1 cup sugar
1/2 cup shortening
1 cup dark molasses
1/2 cup water
4 cups all-purpose flour
1 1/2 teaspoons salt
1 1/2 teaspoons ground ginger
1 teaspoon baking soda
1/2 teaspoon ground cloves
1/2 teaspoon ground nutmeg
1/4 teaspoon ground allspice
Sugar

Mix 1 cup sugar, the shortening, molasses and water in 3-quart bowl. Stir in remaining ingredients except sugar. Cover and refrigerate at least 2 hours.

Heat oven to 375°. Roll dough 1/4 inch thick on well-floured, cloth-covered board. Cut into 3-inch circles; sprinkle with sugar. Place about 1 1/2 inches apart on ungreased cookie sheet. Bake until almost no indentation remains when touched, 10 to 12 minutes. Cool 2 minutes; remove from cookie sheet. Cool completely.

Serving Size: 1 Cookie Calories 125 (Calories from Fat 25); Fat 3 g (Saturated 1 g); Cholesterol 0 mg; Sodium 130 mg; Carbohydrate 24 g; (Dietary Fiber 0 g); Protein 1 g

To Grease or Not to Grease

Greasing cookie sheets isn't necessary for cookie dough that has a lot of shortening in it. If a recipe calls for a greased cookie sheet, use a solid vegetable shortening. Don't use a vegetable oil for greasing; the area between the cookies will burn during baking, which will be almost impossible to clean.

Joe Froggers

Peach Triangles

About 4 dozen cookies

Peach Filling (below)
1 cup sugar
1/2 cup shortening
2 eggs
2 cups all-purpose flour
1 1/2 teaspoons baking powder
1/4 teaspoon salt
Sugar

Heat oven to 375°. Prepare Peach Filling. Mix 1 cup sugar and shortening in large bowl. Stir in eggs. Stir in flour, baking powder and salt.

Roll half of dough at a time 1/8 inch thick on lightly floured, cloth-covered surface. Cut into 3-inch rounds. Place 1 level teaspoon filling in center of each round. Bring three sides of each round together at center to form triangle. Pinch edges together to form slight ridge. Place on ungreased cookie sheet. Sprinkle with sugar. Bake 9 to 12 minutes or until golden brown. Cool slightly; remove from cookie sheet.

Peach Filling

2/3 cup peach preserves
1/2 cup finely chopped dried peaches

Combine ingredients.

Serving Size: 1 Cookie Calories 80 (Calories from Fat 20); Fat 2 g (Saturated 1 g); Cholesterol 10 mg; Sodium 30 mg; Carbohydrate 14 g; (Dietary Fiber 0 g); Protein 1 g

Raspberry Logs

4 dozen cookies

For something different, try substituting your favorite flavor for the raspberry preserves.

1 cup granulated sugar
1/2 cup (1 stick) margarine or butter
1/4 cup shortening
2 teaspoons vanilla
2 eggs
2 1/4 cups all-purpose flour
1/2 cup ground walnuts
1 teaspoon baking powder
1/4 teaspoon salt
1/2 cup raspberry preserves
Powdered sugar

Mix granulated sugar, margarine, shortening, vanilla and eggs in large bowl. Stir in remaining ingredients except preserves and powdered sugar. Cover and refrigerate about 3 hours or until firm.

Heat oven to 375°. Roll half of dough at a time into 12-inch square on floured, cloth-covered surface. Cut into rectangles, 3 × 2 inches. Place 1/2 teaspoon preserves 1/4 inch from edge along one 3-inch side of each rectangle. Fold dough lengthwise over preserves. Seal edges with fork. Place on ungreased cookie sheet. Bake 8 to 10 minutes or until light brown. Remove from cookie sheet. Roll in powdered sugar while warm.

Serving Size: 1 Cookie Calories 90 (Calories from Fat 35); Fat 4 g (Saturated 1 g); Cholesterol 10 mg; Sodium 50 mg; Carbohydrate 12 g; (Dietary Fiber 0 g); Protein 1 g

Toffee Meringue Sticks

About 4 dozen cookies

Shape the dough strips easily this way: Roll one-fourth of the dough into a rope about 10 inches long, then roll and flatten it into a 12 × 3-inch rectangle.

- 1 cup packed brown sugar
- 1/3 cup margarine or butter, softened
- 1 teaspoon vanilla
- 1 egg yolk
- 1/2 cup whipping (heavy) cream
- 2 1/2 cups all-purpose flour
- 1/4 teaspoon salt
- 2 egg whites
- 1/2 cup granulated sugar
- 1 package (6 ounces) almond brickle pieces

Mix brown sugar, margaine, vanilla and egg yolk in large bowl. Stir in whipping cream. Stir in flower and salt. Cover and refrigerate about 1 hour or until firm.

Heat oven to 375°. Roll one-fourth of dough at a time into strip, 12 × 3 inches, on floured surface. Place two strips at a time about 2 inches apart on ungreased cookie sheet.

Beat egg whites in medium bowl on high speed until foamy. Gradually beat in granulated sugar. Continue beating until stiff and glossy. Fold in brickle pieces. Spread one-fourth of the meringue over each strip of dough. Bake 12 to 14 minutes or until edges are light brown. Cool 10 minutes. Cut each strip crosswise into 1-inch sticks. Remove from cookie sheet.

Serving Size: 1 Cookie Calories 90 (Calories from Fat 30); Fat 14 g (Saturated 2 g); Cholesterol 10 mg; Sodium 40 mg; Carbohydrate 14 g; (Dietary Fiber 0 g); Protein 1 g

Chocolate-Cherry Stripe Cookies

About 3 1/2 dozen cookies

- 1 1/2 cups sugar
- 1/2 cup shortening
- 1/2 cup margarine or butter, softened
- 1 teaspoon vanilla
- 1 egg
- 3 cups all-purpose flower
- 1/4 teaspoon salt
- 1/4 cup cocoa
- 2 tablespoons plus 1 teaspoon milk
- 1/3 cup finely chopped maraschino cherries, very well drained

Mix sugar, shortening, margarine, vanilla and egg in large bowl. Stir in flour and salt. Divide dough in half. Mix cocoa and milk into one half and cherries into the other half.

Roll cherry dough into rectangle, 10 × 8 inches, on floured surface, turning over occasionally so dough does not stick. Roll chocolate dough into rectangle, 10 × 8 inches, on waxed paper. Place chocolate rectangle on top of cherry rectangle and remove waxed paper. Cut in half lengthwise. Stack layers, being careful to alternate colors; repeat. Wrap and refrigerate about 2 hours or until firm.

Heat oven to 375°. cut dough crosswise into 1/4-inch slices. Place 2 inches apart on ungreased cookie sheet. Bake 9 to 11 minutes or until edges begin to brown. Cool slightly; remove from cookie sheet.

Serving Size: 1 Cookie Calories 110 (Calories from Fat 45); Fat 5 g (Saturated 1 g); Cholesterol 5 mg; Sodium 40 mg; Carbohydrate 15 g; (Dietary Fiber 0 g); Protein 1 g

Stack layers of dough being careful to alternate colors.

Repeat cutting lengthwise and stacking.

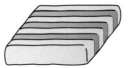

Cut dough crosswise into slices.

Animal Cookies

3

Molded Cookies

Animal Cookies

About 1 1/2 dozen cookies

These cookies are a terrific solution to rainy-day blues. If the dough softens too much, cover and refrigerate until firm (about 1 hour).

1/2 cup granulated sugar
1/2 cup packed brown sugar
1/2 cup (1 stick) margarine or butter, softened
1 teaspoon vanilla
1 egg
2 cups all-purpose flour
1 teaspoon baking powder
1/2 teaspoon salt
1/2 teaspoon ground cinnamon

Heat oven to 350°. Mix sugars, margarine, vanilla and egg in large bowl. Stir in remaining ingredients. (If dough is too soft to shape, cover and refrigerate about 2 hours or until firm.)

Shape dough 2 tablespoons at a time into slightly flattened balls and ropes. Arrange on ungreased cookie sheet to form animals as desired. Bake about 10 to 12 minutes or until edges are golden brown.

LETTER AND NUMBER COOKIES: Prepare dough as directed. Shape level tablespoonfuls of dough into ropes, about 8 inches long and about 1/4 inch thick. Shape into letters and numbers as desired on ungreased cookie sheet. Bake 8 to 10 minutes. Cool 3 minutes; remove from cookie sheet.   **About 3 dozen cookies**

Serving Size: 1 Cookie Calories 160 (Calories from Fat 55); Fat 6 g (Saturated 1 g); Cholesterol 13 mg; Sodium 170 mg; Carbohydrate 25 g; (Dietary Fiber 0 g); Protein 2 g

Arrange balls or rope of dough on cookie sheet to form animals as desired.

Gingersnaps

About 4 dozen cookies

You can use either light or dark molasses in this recipe. Light molasses will give you a spicier cookie.

    1 cup packed brown sugar
    3/4 cup shortening
    1/4 cup molasses
    1 egg
    2 1/4 cups all-purpose flour
    2 teaspoons baking soda
    1 teaspoon ground cinnamon
    1 teaspoon ground ginger
    1/2 teaspoon ground cloves
    1/4 teaspoon salt
    Granulated sugar

Mix brown sugar, shortening, molasses and egg. Stir in flour, baking soda, cinnamon, ginger, cloves and salt. Cover and refrigerate at least 1 hour.

Heat oven to 375°. Grease cookie sheet lightly. Shape dough by rounded teaspoonfuls into balls. Dip tops into granulated sugar. Place balls, sugared sides up, about 3 inches apart on cookie sheet. Bake 10 to 12 minutes or just until set; cool.

Serving Size: 1 Cookie Calories 80 (Calories from Fat 25); Fat 3 g (Saturated 1 g); Cholesterol 5 mg; Sodium 65 mg; Carbohydrate 12 g; (Dietary Fiber 0 g); Protein 1 g

Peanut Butter Cookies

About 3 dozen cookies

For a sweet change, try dipping the fork in sugar instead of flour.

    1/2 cup granulated sugar
    1/2 cup packed brown sugar
    1/2 cup peanut butter
    1/4 cup shortening
    1/4 cup (1/2 stick) margarine or butter, softened
    1 egg
    1 1/4 cups all-purpose flour
    3/4 teaspoon baking soda
    1/2 teaspoon baking powder

Mix sugars, peanut butter, shortening, margarine and egg. Stir in remaining ingredients. Cover and refrigerate at least 3 hours.

Heat oven to 375°. Shape dough into 1 1/4-inch balls. Place about 3 inches apart on ungreased cookie sheet. Flatten in crisscross pattern with fork dipped in flour. Bake 9 to 10 minutes or until light brown. Cool 2 minutes; remove from cookie sheet.

Serving Size: 1 Cookie Calories 90 (Calories from Fat 45); Fat 5 g (Saturated 1 g); Cholesterol 5 mg; Sodium 70 mg; Carbohydrate 10 g; (Dietary Fiber 0 g); Protein 1 g

---

Slicing Magic

Use dental floss to cut refrigerator-cookie dough into slices. The dough cuts easily and cleanly, without any ragged edges.

Chocolate Cookie Slices

About 8 dozen cookies

1 1/2 cups powdered sugar
1 1/4 cups (2 1/2 sticks) margarine or butter, softened
1 egg
3 cups all-purpose flour
1/2 cup cocoa
1/4 teaspoon salt
1 1/2 cups finely chopped pecans
Fudge Frosting (below)

Mix powdered sugar, margarine and egg. Stir in flour, cocoa and salt. Cover and refrigerate 1 hour.

Divide into halves. Shape each half into roll, about 1 1/2 inches in diameter. Roll in pecans. Wrap and refrigerate at least 8 hours but no longer than 6 weeks.

Heat oven to 400°. Cut rolls into 1/8-inch slices. (If dough crumbles while cutting, let warm slightly.) Place about 1 inch apart on ungreased cookie sheet. Bake about 8minutes. Remove immediately from cookie sheet; cool. Frost with Fudge Frosting, if desired.

FUDGE FROSTING

1 cup sugar
1/3 cup milk
1/4 cup shortening
2 ounces unsweetened chocolate
1/4 teaspoon salt
1 teaspoon vanilla

Heat sugar, milk, shortening, chocolate and salt to rolling boil, stirring occasionally. Boil 1 minute without stirring. Place pan in bowl of ice and water. Beat until thick and cold; stir in vanilla.

Serving Size: 1 Cookie Calories 80 (Calories from Fat 45); Fat 5 g (Saturated 1 g); Cholesterol 2 mg; Sodium 40 mg; Carbohydrate 8 g; (Dietary Fiber 0 g); Protein 1 g

Vanilla Cookie Slices

About 7 dozen cookies

1 cup sugar
1 cup (2 sticks) margarine or butter, softened
2 eggs
1 1/2 teaspoons vanilla
3 cups all-purpose flour
1 teaspoon salt
1/2 teaspoon baking soda

Mix sugar, margarine, eggs and vanilla. Stir in remaining ingredients. Divide into three equal parts. Shape each part into roll, about 1 1/2 inches in diameter. Wrap and refrigerate at least 4 hours, but no longer than 6 weeks.

Heat oven to 400°. Cut rolls into 1/8-inch slices. Place about 1 inch apart on ungreased cookie sheet. Bake 8 to 10 minutes. Remove immediately from cookie sheet.

CINNAMON SLICES: Substitute 1/2 cup packed brown sugar for 1/2 cup of the granulated sugar and 1 tablespoon ground cinnamon for the vanilla.

COOKIE TARTS: Spoon 1 teaspoon jelly or preserves onto half the slices; top with remaining slices. Seal edges. Cut slits in tops so filling shows. **About 3 1/2 dozen tarts.**

ORANGE-ALMOND SLICES: Mix in 1 tablespoon grated orange peel with the margarine and 1/2 cup cut-up blanched almonds with the flour.

PEANUT BUTTER SLICES: Substitute packed dark brown sugar for the granulated sugar and 1/2 cup crunchy peanut butter for 1/2 cup of the softened margarine.

WALNUT SLICES: Stir in 1/2 cup chopped black walnuts.

WHOLE WHEAT SLICES: Substitute whole wheat flour for the all-purpose flour.

Serving Size: 1 Cookie Calories 50 (Calories from Fat 20); Fat 2 g (Saturated 1 g); Cholesterol 5 mg; Sodium 65 mg; Carbohydrate 7 g; (Dietary Fiber 0 g); Protein 1 g

Chocolate-Peppermint Refrigerator Cookies

4 dozen cookies

1 1/2 cups powdered sugar
1 cup (2 sticks) margarine or butter, softened
1 egg
2 2/3 cups all-purpose flour
1/4 teaspoon salt
1/4 cup cocoa
1 tablespoon milk
1/4 cup finely crushed peppermint candy

Mix powdered sugar, margarine and egg in large bowl. Stir in flour and salt. Divide dough in half. Stir cocoa and milk into one half and peppermint candy into other half.

Shape chocolate dough into rectangle, 12 × 6 1/2 inches, on waxed paper. Shape peppermint dough into roll, 12 inches long; place on chocolate dough. Wrap chocolate dough around peppermint dough using waxed paper to help lift. Press edges together. Wrap and refrigerate about 2 hours or until firm.

Heat oven to 375°. Cut rolls into 1/4-inch slices. Place about 1 inch apart on ungreased cookie sheet. Bake 8 to 10 minutes or until set. Remove from cookie sheet.

CHOCOLATE-WINTERGREEN REFRIGER-ATOR COOKIES: Omit peppermint candies. Stir 1/4 cup chocolate shot, 1/4 teaspoon wintergreen extract and 4 drops green food color into plain dough. Continue as directed.

Serving Size: 1 Cookie Calories 80 (Calories from Fat 35); Fat 4 g (Saturated 1 g); Cholesterol 5 mg; Sodium 60 mg; Carbohydrate 10 g; (Dietary Fiber 0 g); Protein 1 g

Peanut Butter-Chocolate Kisses

About 3 dozen cookies

1/2 cup granulated sugar
1/2 cup packed brown sugar
1/2 cup creamy peanut butter
1/4 cup (1/2 stick) margarine or butter, softened
1/4 cup shortening
1 egg
1 1/2 cups all-purpose flour
3/4 teaspoon baking soda
1/2 teaspoon baking powder
Granulated sugar
About 3 dozen milk chocolate candy kisses or stars or desired amount chocolate-coated peanut candies

Heat oven to 375°. Mix 1/2 cup granulated sugar, the brown sugar, peanut butter, margarine, shortening and egg thoroughly. Stir in flour, baking soda and baking powder. Mold dough into 1-inch balls; roll in sugar. Place about 2 inches apart on ungreased cookie sheet. Bake until edges are light brown, 8 to 10 minutes. Immediately press candy kiss firmly in each cookie; cool.

Serving Size: 1 Cookie Calories 120 (Calories from Fat 55); Fat 6 g (Saturated 2 g); Cholesterol 5 mg; Sodium 70 mg; Carbohydrate 15 g; (Dietary Fiber 0 g); Protein 2 g

No More Sticky Fingers

Cookie dough sticking to your hands? Try this quick trick: Wet your hands with cold water occasionally when shaping cookie dough into balls and the dough won't stick to your palms. This is especially helpful for doughs with a lot of shortening.

Raspberry Jam Strips

60 strips

1 cup (2 sticks) margarine or butter, softened
1/2 cup granulated sugar
1/2 cup packed brown sugar
1 egg
1 teaspoon vanilla
2 1/2 cups all-purpose flour
1 teaspoon baking powder
1/2 cup raspberry jam
Almond Glaze (below)

Mix margarine, sugars, egg and vanilla. Stir in flour and baking powder. (If dough is soft, cover and refrigerate at least 1 hour.)

Heat oven to 350°. Divide dough into eight equal parts. Mold each part into strip, 8 × 1 1/2 inches, on ungreased cookie sheet. Make slight indentation down center of each with handle of wooden spoon; fill with about 1 1/2 teaspoons jam. Bake until edges are light brown, 10 to 12 minutes. Cool slightly. Drizzle with Almond Glaze. Cut diagonally into 1-inch pieces.

ALMOND GLAZE

1 cup powdered sugar
1/2 teaspoon almond extract
2 to 3 teaspoons water

Beat powdered sugar, almond extract and water until smooth and of desired consistency.

Serving Size: 1 Strip Calories 75 (Calories from Fat 25); Fat 3 g (Saturated 1 g); Cholesterol 5 mg; Sodium 45 mg; Carbohydrate 11 g; (Dietary Fiber 0 g); Protein 1 g

Lemon Cookie Sandwiches

About 4 dozen cookies

1/2 cup sugar
1/2 cup (1 stick) margarine or butter, softened
1 tablespoon water
1 teaspoon vanilla
2 eggs, separated
1 1/2 cups all-purpose flour
1/2 teaspoon salt
1/4 teaspoon baking soda
2/3 cup finely chopped nuts
Lemon Filling (below)

Mix sugar, margarine, water, vanilla and egg yolks. Stir in flour, salt and baking soda. Divide dough into halves. Shape each half into roll, about 1 1/2 inches in diameter and about 7 inches long. Wrap and refrigerate at least 4 hours.

Heat oven to 400°. Cut rolls into 1/8-inch slices. Place about 1 inch apart on ungreased cookie sheet. Beat egg whites slightly; stir in nuts. Spoon 1/2 teaspoon nut mixture onto half the cookie slices. Bake until edges begin to brown, about 6 minutes. Remove immediately from cookie sheet; cool. Put nut-topped and plain cookies together in pairs with Lemon Filling, placing the nut-topped cookies on top.

LEMON FILLING

1 cup powdered sugar
2 teaspoons margarine or butter, softened
1 teaspoon grated lemon peel
1 tablespoon plus 1 1/2 teaspoons lemon juice

Beat all ingredients until smooth.

Serving Size: 1 Cookie Calories 65 (Calories from Fat 25); Fat 3 g (Saturated 0 g); Cholesterol 10 mg; Sodium 55 mg; Carbohydrate 8 g; (Dietary Fiber 0 g); Protein 1 g

Hungarian Poppy Seed Cookies/Mint Ravioli Cookies

Mint Ravioli Cookies

3 dozen cookies

1/2 cup (1 stick) margarine or butter, softened
1/2 cup shortening
1 cup sugar
1 egg
2 1/2 cups all-purpose flour
1 teaspoon baking powder
1/4 teaspoon salt
3 dozen rectangular chocolate mints

Mix margarine, shortening, sugar and egg in large bowl. Stir in flour, baking powder and salt. Cover and refrigerate about 1 hour or until firm.

Heat oven to 400°. Roll half of dough into rectangle, 13 × 9 inches, on floured surface. Place mints on dough, forming six uniform rows of 6. Roll remaining dough into rectangle, 13 × 9 inches, on floured waxed paper. Place over mint-covered dough and remove waxed paper. Cut between mints with pastry wheel or knife and press edges with fork to seal. Bake on ungreased cookie sheet 7 to 9 minutes or until light brown. Remove from cookie sheet.

Serving Size: 1 Cookie Calories 125 (Calories from Fat 65); Fat 7 g (Saturated 2 g); Cholesterol 5 mg; Sodium 65 mg; Carbohydrate 15 g; (Dietary Fiber 0 g); Protein 1 g

Place mints on dough, forming six rows of 6.

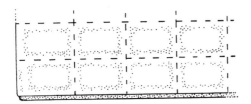

Place remaining dough over mint-covered dough; cut between mints.

Hungarian Poppy Seed Cookies

About 3 dozen cookies

Lemon peel, clove and poppy seed often flavor Eastern European cookies. Look for commercially prepared poppy seed filling next to canned pie fillings at the supermarket.

1/2 cup (1 stick) margarine or butter, softened
1/4 cup granulated sugar
1 teaspoon grated lemon peel
1 egg
1 1/4 cups all-purpose flour
1/2 teaspoon baking soda
1/4 teaspoon ground cloves
3/4 cup poppy seed filling
Powdered sugar

Beat margarine and granulated sugar in large bowl until light and fluffy. Beat in lemon peel and egg. Stir in flour, baking soda and cloves. Roll dough between pieces of waxed paper into 1/4-inch-thick rectangle, 12 × 10 inches. Refrigerate 30 minutes or until firm.

Heat oven to 350°. Grease cookie sheet. Remove waxed paper from one side of dough. Spread poppy seed filling to within 1/4 inch of edges. Roll up tightly, beginning at 12-inch side, peeling off waxed paper as dough is rolled. Pinch edge of dough to seal well. Cut dough into 1/2-inch slices. Place on cookie sheet about 1 inch apart. Bake 10 to 12 minutes or until edges are light brown. Cool slightly; remove from cookie sheet. Sprinkle with powdered sugar.

Serving Size: 1 Cookie Calories 80 (Calories from Fat 35); Fat 4 g (Saturated 1 g); Cholesterol 5 mg; Sodium 50 mg; Carbohydrate 10 g; (Dietary Fiber 0 g); Protein 1 g

Cocoa Mini-Meringues (p. 48)

4

Fancy Treats

Hazelnut Sablés

About 3 dozen cookies

Pronounced "sah-blay," sablés are French cookies that translate to "sandies." They are rich, short cookies with pronounced hazelnut flavor.

3/4 cup (1 1/2 sticks) margarine or butter, softened
3/4 cup powdered sugar
1/2 teaspoon vanilla
1 egg yolk
1 1/4 cups all-purpose flour
1/2 cup hazelnuts, toasted and ground
1 egg, beaten
1/4 cup chopped hazelnuts
1/4 cup sanding sugar

Beat margarine and powdered sugar in large bowl until light and fluffy. Stir in vanilla and egg yolk. Stir in flour and ground hazelnuts until well blended. Cover tightly and refrigerate 1 hour.

Heat oven to 350°. Roll one-fourth of dough at a time 1/4 inch thick on lightly floured surface. (Keep remaining dough refrigerated until ready to roll.) Cut into 2 1/2-inch rounds. Place about 2 inches apart on ungreased cookie sheet. Brush with egg. Sprinkle with chopped hazelnuts and sugar. Bake 8 to 10 minutes or until edges are light brown. Remove from cookie sheet.

Serving Size: 1 Cookie Calories 80 (Calories from Fat 45); Fat 5 g (Saturated 1 g); Cholesterol 10 mg; Sodium 45 mg; Carbohydrate 8 g; (Dietary Fiber 0 g); Protein 1 g

Florentines

About 5 dozen cookies

1/4 cup sugar

3/4 cup whipping cream

1/4 cup all-purpose flour

1/2 cup slivered almonds, very finely chopped

8 ounces candied orange peel, very finely chopped

2 bars (4 or 8 ounces each) sweet cooking chocolate, cut into pieces

Heat oven to 350°. Blend sugar and cream. Stir in flour, almonds and orange peel. (Mixture will be thin.) Drop by teaspoonfuls onto heavily greased and floured cookie sheet. Spread mixture into thin circles with knife or spatula.

Bake just until edges are light brown, 10 to 12 minutes. Let cool a few minutes before removing from cookie sheet; cool. Melt chocolate over low heat, stirring constantly, until melted. Turn cookies upside down; spread with chocolate. Let stand at room temperature until chocolate is firm, at least 3 hours. Store in covered container at room temperature or refrigerate.

Serving Size: 1 Cookie Calories 55 (Calories from Fat 25); Fat 3 g (Saturated 1 g); Cholesterol 5 mg; Sodium 0 mg; Carbohydrate 7 g; (Dietary Fiber 0 g); Protein 0 g

Pizzelles

About 3 1/2 dozen cookies

You can also use a krumkake iron to make these crisp Italian cookies.

2 cups all-purpose flour

1 cup sugar

2 teaspoons baking powder

3/4 cup (1 1/2 sticks) margarine or butter, melted and cooled

1 tablespoon anise extract or vanilla

4 eggs, slightly beaten

Grease pizzelle iron. Heat pizzelle iron according to manufacturer's directions. Mix all ingredients. Drop 1 tablespoon batter onto heated pizzelle iron and close iron. Bake about 30 seconds or until golden brown. Carefully remove pizzelle from iron; cool. Repeat with remaining batter.

Serving Size: 1 Cookie Calories 80 (Calories from Fat 35); Fat 4 g (Saturated 1 g); Cholesterol 20 mg; Sodium 70 mg; Carbohydrate 10 g; (Dietary Fiber 0 g); Protein 1 g

French Lace Cookies

About 4 dozen cookies

This elegant cookie can also be served as a rolled variation. While cookies are still warm, roll them around the handle of a wooden spoon. If one should break during rolling, the cookies are too cool; return them to the oven for a minute to soften, then try again.

1/2 cup light corn syrup

1/2 cup shortening

2/3 cup packed brown sugar

1 cup all-purpose flour

1 cup finely chopped pecans

Heat oven to 375°. Grease cookie sheet lightly. Heat corn syrup, shortening and brown sugar to boiling in 2-quart saucepan over medium heat, stirring constantly; remove from heat. Gradually stir in flour and pecans. Drop batter by teaspoonfuls about 3 inches apart onto cookie sheet. (Keep batter warm by placing saucepan over hot water; bake only 8 or 9 cookies at a time.) Bake about 5 minutes or until set. Cool 3 to 5 minutes; remove from cookie sheet. Drizzle with melted chocolate, if desired.

Serving Size: 1 Cookie Calories 70 (Calories from Fat 35); Fat 4 g (Saturated 1 g); Cholesterol 0 mg; Sodium 5 mg; Carbohydrate 8 g; (Dietary Fiber 0 g); Protein 0 g

French Lace Cookies, Pizzelles

Cream Wafers

About 5 dozen sandwich cookies

For variety, tint portions of the filling different colors.

  2 cups all-purpose flour
  1 cup (2 sticks) margarine or butter, softened
  1/3 cup whipping (heavy) cream
  Sugar
  Creamy Filling (below)

Mix flour, margarine and whipping cream. Cover and refrigerate about 1 hour or until firm.

Heat oven to 375°. Roll one-third of dough at a time 1/8 inch thick on floured surface. (Keep remaining dough refrigerated until ready to roll.) Cut into 1 1/2-inch rounds. Generously cover large piece waxed paper with sugar. Using spatula, transfer rounds to waxed paper. Turn each round to coat both sides. Place on ungreased cookie sheet. Prick each round with fork about 4 times.

Bake 7 to 9 minutes or just until set but not brown. Remove from cookie sheet. Cool completely. Prepare Creamy Filling. Put cookies together in pairs with about 1/2 teaspoon filling each.

CREAMY FILLING

  3/4 cup powdered sugar
  1/4 cup (1/2 stick) margarine or butter, softened
  1 teaspoon vanilla
  Food color, if desired

Mix all ingredients until smooth. Add few drops water, if necessary.

Serving Size: 1 Cookie Calories 90 (Calories from Fat 55); Fat 6 g (Saturated 1 g); Cholesterol 2 mg; Sodium 60 mg; Carbohydrate 9 g; (Dietary Fiber 0 g); Protein 0 g

Cream Squares

About 4 dozen cookies

  2 eggs
  1 cup sugar
  1 cup whipping (heavy) cream
  4 cups all-purpose flour
  3 teaspoons baking powder
  1 teaspoon salt

Beat eggs in large bowl until foamy. Gradually beat in sugar. Stir in whipping cream. Stir in flour, baking powder and salt. Cover and refrigerate about 2 hours or until firm.

Heat oven to 375°. Grease cookie sheet. Roll half of dough at a time into rectangle 12 × 8 inches, on floured surface. Cut into 2-inch squares. Place 2 inches apart on cookie sheet. Make two 1/2-inch cuts on all sides of each square. Bake 10 to 13 minutes or until edges are light brown. Remove from cookie sheet.

Serving Size: 1 Cookie Calories 70 (Calories from Fat 20); Fat 2 g (Saturated 1 g); Cholesterol 15 mg; Sodium 80 mg; Carbohydrate 12 g; (Dietary Fiber 0 g); Protein 1 g

Cookie Clinic

Always bake a test cookie first to make sure the cookies will come out right. If the cookie spreads more than desired, add 1 to 2 tablespoons flour to the dough. If the dough is too dry, mix in 1 to 2 tablespoons milk until the dough holds together. Do not overmix dough after flour has been added, or cookies will be tough.

Cream Wafers, Cream Squares

Cocoa Mini-Meringues

48 meringues

3 egg whites
1/4 teaspoon cream of tartar
3/4 cup sugar
2 tablespoons cocoa
1 cup whipping (heavy) cream, whipped
Small fresh fruit pieces or berries (about
150 pieces)

Heat oven to 275°. Cover cookie sheets with aluminum foil or cooking parchment paper. Beat egg whites and cream of tartar in medium bowl until foamy. Beat in sugar, 1 tablespoon at a time; beat until stiff and glossy. Do not underbeat. Sprinkle cocoa on meringue and gently fold in.

Drop meringue by level measuring tablespoonfuls about 1 1/2 inches apart onto baking sheets, making 48 meringues. Make small indentation in center of each with tip of teaspoon. Bake 10 minutes. Turn off oven; leave meringues in oven with door closed 1 hour. Remove from oven; finish cooling meringues away from draft.

Top each meringue with 1 teaspoon whipped cream and 2 or 3 fresh fruit pieces or berries.

Serving Size: 1 Meringue Calories 35 (Calories from Fat 20); Fat 2 g (Saturated 1 g); Cholesterol 5 mg; Sodium 5 mg; Carbohydrate 4 g; (Dietary Fiber 0 g); Protein 0 g

Lemon Tea Biscuits

4 dozen sandwich cookies

Assemble these light wafers with the tart lemon filling no longer than an hour or two before serving—they soften on standing. For fun, try cutting the dough into hearts, diamonds, clubs and spades.

1 cup (2 sticks) margarine or butter, softened
1/2 cup sugar
1 tablespoon grated lemon peel
1/4 teaspoon salt
1 egg
2 cups all-purpose flour
1/2 cup ground pecans
1 cup lemon curd or pie filling
Lemon Glaze (below)

Mix margarine, sugar, lemon peel, salt and egg in large bowl until well blended. Stir in flour and pecans. Cover and refrigerate 1 hour or until firm.

Heat oven to 350°. Roll half of dough at a time about 1/8 inch thick on floured surface. Cut into 2-inch rounds. Place on ungreased cookie sheet. Bake 7 to 9 minutes or until edges are just barely brown. Remove from cookie sheet. Cool completely. Put cookies together in pairs using rounded teaspoonful lemon curd for filling. Prepare Lemon Glaze and brush on tops of cookies.

LEMON GLAZE

1/4 cup powdered sugar
1 teaspoon grated lemon peel
2 teaspoons lemon juice

Mix all ingredients.

Serving Size: 1 Cookie Calories 80 (Calories from Fat 45); Fat 5 g (Saturated 1 g); Cholesterol 10 mg; Sodium 65 mg; Carbohydrate 8 g; (Dietary Fiber 0 g); Protein 1 g

Chocolate Bonbon Cookies

About 20 to 25 cookies

3/4 cup powdered sugar
1/2 cup margarine or butter, softened
1 tablespoon vanilla
1 square (1 ounce) unsweetened chocolate, melted
1 1/2 cups all-purpose flour
1/8 teaspoon salt
Dates, nuts, semisweet chocolate chips and candied or maraschino cherries
Vanilla Glaze or Chocolate Glaze (below)

Heat oven to 350°. Mix powdered sugar, margarine, vanilla and chocolate. Work in flour and salt until dough holds together. (If dough is dry mix in 1 to 2 tablespoons milk.)

Mold dough by tablespoonfuls around date, nut, chocolate chips or cherry. Place cookies about 1 inch apart on ungreased cookie sheet. Bake until set but not brown, 12 to 15 minutes; cool. Dip tops of cookies into Vanilla Glaze. Decorate each with coconut, nuts, colored sugar, chocolate chips or chocolate shot if desired.

VANILLA GLAZE

Mix 1 cup powdered sugar, 1 tablespoon plus 1 1/2 teaspoons milk and 1 teaspoon vanilla. Stir in few drops food color.

CHOCOLATE GLAZE

1/2 cup semisweet chocolate chips
2 tablespoons margarine or butter
2 tablespoons water
1/2 cup powdered sugar

Heat chocolate chips, margarine and water over low heat, stirring constantly, until melted. Remove from heat; stir in powdered sugar until smooth.

Serving Size: 1 Cookie Calories 140 (Calories from Fat 55); Fat 6 g (Saturated 2 g); Cholesterol 0 mg; Sodium 70 mg; Carbohydrate 21 g; (Dietary Fiber 0 g); Protein 1 g

Baklava Puffs

32 puffs

1 cup very finely chopped pecans, walnuts or almonds
1/3 cup honey
1/2 teaspoon ground cinnamon
1 package (17 1/4 ounces) frozen puff pastry sheets, thawed
2 tablespoons honey
3 tablespoons very finely chopped pecans, walnuts or almonds

Heat oven to 425°. Mix 1 cup pecans, 1/3 cup honey and the cinnamon; reserve. Roll each pastry sheet into 10-inch square on lightly floured surface. Cut into 2 1/2-inch squares. Place about 1 teaspoon pecan mixture in center of each square. Moisten edges of squares with water; fold in half to form triangle. Press edges to seal. Place on ungreased cookie sheet.

Bake 13 to 15 minutes or until puffy and golden brown. Heat 2 tablespoons honey until warm and slightly thinned. Lightly brush honey on warm puffs. Sprinkle with 3 tablespoons pecans.

Serving Size: 1 Puff Calories 135 (Calories from Fat 44); Fat 10 g (Saturated 3 g); Cholesterol 5 mg; Sodium 35 mg; Carbohydrate 10 g; (Dietary Fiber 0 g); Protein 1 g

Truffle Cookies

Truffle Cookies

About 2 dozen cookies

6 squares (1 ounce each) unsweetened chocolate, cut up
2 tablespoons margarine or butter
1/3 cup half-and-half
1/2 cup powdered sugar
1/2 cup (1 stick) margarine or butter, softened
3/4 cup powdered sugar
1 tablespoon vanilla
1 square (1 ounce) unsweetened chocolate, melted and cooled
1 1/2 cups all-purpose flour
1/8 teaspoon salt
Chocolate Icing (below)

Heat 6 squares unsweetened chocolate in 2-quart heavy saucepan over low heat, stirring constantly, until melted. Remove from heat; stir in 2 tablespoons margarine, the half-and-half and 1/2 cup powdered sugar. Shape mixture into 1-inch balls; freeze 30 minutes to set.

Heat oven to 350°. Mix 1/2 cup margarine, 3/4 cup powdered sugar, the vanilla and 1 square unsweetened chocolate. Work in flour and salt until dough holds together. (If dough is dry, mix in 1 or 2 tablespoons of milk.) Mold portions of dough around frozen chocolate balls to form 1 1/2-inch balls. Place about 1 inch apart on ungreased cookie sheet. Bake 12 to 15 minutes or until set but not brown.

Cool; dip tops of cookies into Chocolate Icing. If desired, sprinkle with finely chopped nuts or chocolate shot or drizzle with melted chocolate or vanilla-flavored candy coating.

CHOCOLATE ICING

Mix 1 cup powdered sugar, 2 tablespoons milk and 1 square (1 ounce) melted unsweetened chocolate (cool) until smooth.

Serving Size: 1 Cookie Calories 170 (Calories from Fat 90); Fat 10 g (Saturated 4 g); Cholesterol 0 mg; Sodium 70 mg; Carbohydrate 20 g; (Dietary Fiber 2 g); Protein 2 g

Petticoat Tails

About 6 dozen cookies

When this recipe was brought from France to Scotland, the French name was *petits gateaux tailles* (translated as "little cakes cut off"). But the English could not pronounce it correctly; the name was corrupted, and they were called as they *sounded* to the Scotch or English ear: "petticoat tails."

1 cup powdered sugar
1 cup (2 sticks) margarine or butter, softened
2 1/2 cups all-purpose flour
1/4 teaspoon salt
1 teaspoon vanilla or 1/2 teaspoon almond extract

Mix powdered sugar and butter in medium bowl. Stir in remaining ingredients, using hands if necessary. Shape dough into roll about 9 inches long. Wrap and refrigerate at least 2 hours.

Heat oven to 400°. Cut roll into 1/8-inch slices. Place slices about 1 inch apart on ungreased cookie sheet. Bake 6 to 8 minutes or until light brown. Cool slightly; remove from cookie sheet.

Serving Size: 1 Cookie Calories 45 (Calories from Fat 25); Fat 3 g (Saturated 2 g); Cholesterol 5 mg; Sodium 25 mg; Carbohydrate 5 g; (Dietary Fiber 0 g); Protein 0 g

Viva Vanilla!

An easy way to measure vanilla is to use the bottle cap. The cap on a small bottle is about 1/2 teaspoon; the cap on a 4-ounce bottle equals 1 teaspoon.

Gingerbread Village (p. 54)

5

Holiday Cookies

Gingerbread People

About 2 1/2 dozen 2 1/2-inch cookies

Queen Elizabeth of England is credited with creating gingerbread people in the sixteenth century when she ordered cakes spiced with ginger to be baked in the shapes of her friends.

1 cup packed brown sugar
1/3 cup shortening
1 1/2 cups dark molasses
2/3 cups cold water
7 cups all-purpose flour
2 teaspoons baking soda
2 teaspoons ground ginger
1/2 teaspoon salt
1 teaspoon ground allspice
1 teaspoon ground cloves
1 teaspoon ground cinnamon

Mix brown sugar, shortening, molasses and water. Stir in remaining ingredients. Cover and refrigerate at least 2 hours.

Heat oven to 350°. Grease cookie sheet lightly. Roll about one-fourth of the dough 1/4 inch thick on floured board. Cut with floured gingerbread cutter or other favorite cutter. Place about 2 inches apart on cookie sheet. Bake 10 to 12 minutes or until no indentation remains when touched; cool. Decorate with colored frosting, colored sugar and candies, if desired.

Serving Size: 1 Cookie Calories 195 (Calories from Fat 25); Fat 3 g (Saturated 1 g); Cholesterol 0 mg; Sodium 130 mg; Carbohydrate 40 g; (Dietary Fiber 1 g); Protein 3 g

Gingerbread Village

One 4-building village

It's fun to populate your village with gingerbread people—trees or other accessory pieces. If using cutters less than 2 inches—check cookies a few minutes before minimum time.

1/2 cup packed brown sugar
1/4 cup shortening
3/4 cup dark molasses
1/3 cup cold water
3 1/2 cups all-purpose flour
1 teaspoon baking soda
1 teaspoon ground ginger
1/2 teaspoon salt
1/2 teaspoon ground allspice
1/2 teaspoon ground cloves
1/2 teaspoon ground cinnamon
Cardboard, about 28 × 10 inches
Aluminum foil or nonabsorbent gift wrap
Frosting (below)
Assorted candies, cookies, nuts and chewy fruit snack in 3-foot rolls

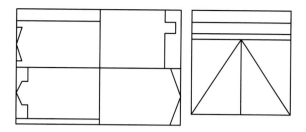

Cut jelly roll into fourths and then into buildings.   *Cut square into braces.*

Heat oven to 350°. Grease square pan, 9 × 9 × 2 inches, and jelly roll pan, 15 1/2 × 10 1/2 × 1 inch. Mix brown sugar, shortening and molasses in large bowl. Stir in cold water. Stir in flour, baking soda, ginger, salt, allspice, cloves and cinnamon.

Press one-third of dough into square pan. Press remaining dough into jelly roll pan. Bake 1 pan at a time about 15 minutes or until no indentation remains when touched in center. Cool 5 minutes. Invert onto large cutting surface. Immediately cut jelly roll into fourths and then into buildings as shown in diagram. Cut square into braces as shown. Cool completely.

Cover cardboard with aluminum foil. Decorate fronts of buildings as desired, using Frosting and assorted candies. Use Frosting to attach braces to backs of buildings, buildings to cardboard and sidewalk to cardboard. Complete by decorating as desired.

FROSTING

2 cups powdered sugar
1/3 cup shortening
2 tablespoons light corn syrup
5 to 6 teaspoons milk
Few drops food color, if desired

Beat all ingredients until smooth and of spreading consistency.

Christmas Cookie Slices

About 7 dozen cookies

Fun different cookies—all from one basic recipe!

1 cup sugar
1 cup (2 sticks) margarine or butter, softened
2 eggs
1 1/2 teaspoons vanilla
3 cups all-purpose flour
1/2 teaspoon salt
1/2 teaspoon baking soda

Mix sugar, margarine, eggs and vanilla. Stir in remaining ingredients. Divide into 3 equal parts. Shape each part into roll, about 1 1/2 inches in diameter. Wrap and refrigerate at least 4 hours.

Heat oven to 400°. Cut rolls into 1/8-inch slices. Place about 1 inch apart on ungreased cookie sheet. Bake until edges begin to brown, 8 to 10 minutes. Immediately remove from cookie sheet.

CHRISTMAS TREES: Shape roll into triangle. Coat sides with green sugar. Continue as directed. Cut tree trunks from several slices; attach trunks to trees on cookie sheet, overlapping slightly.

COOKIE TARTS: Cut out centers of half the unbaked cookies with 3/4-inch cutters, or design your own patterns. Spoon 1/2 teaspoon red jelly or jam onto uncut slices; top with cutout slices. Press edges to seal.

HOLIDAY SUGAR SLICES: Coat rolls with red or green sugar or multicolored candies.

NUTMEG SLICES: Add 1/2 teaspoon ground nutmeg with the flour. Coat rolls with mixture of 1/4 cup sugar and 1/2 teaspoon ground nutmeg.

NUTTY SLICES: Coat rolls with chopped nuts.

PEPPERMINT PINWHEELS: Decrease vanilla to 1 teaspoon; add 1 teaspoon peppermint extract. After dough is mixed, divide into halves. Stir 1/2 teaspoon red or green food color into one half. Cover both halves and refrigerate 1 hour. Roll plain dough into rectangle, about 16 × 9 inches, on lightly floured surface. Repeat with colored dough; place on plain dough. Roll doughs together about 1/4 inch thick. Roll up tightly, beginning at 16-inch side. Wrap and refrigerate. Continue as directed.

RIBBON BAR COOKIES: Decrease vanilla to 1 teaspoon; add 1 teaspoon peppermint extract. After dough is mixed, divide into halves. Stir 1/2 teaspoon red or green food color into one half. Cover both halves and refrigerate 1 hour. Shape each half into 2 strips, each about 9 × 2 1/2 inches, on very lightly floured surface. Layer strips, alternating colors; press together. Wrap and refrigerate. Continue as directed. **About 5 1/2 dozen cookies**

Serving Size: **1 Cookie** Calories 45 (Calories from Fat 20); Fat 2 g (Saturated 0 g); Cholesterol 5 mg; Sodium 45 mg; Carbohydrate 6 g; (Dietary Fiber 0 g); Protein 1 g

Candy Cane Cookies

About 4 1/2 dozen cookies

While red and white are the traditional colors for candy canes, feel free to create candy canes of different colors. Paste food color will give you more intense color.

2 tablespoons crushed peppermint candies
2 tablespoons sugar
1 cup sugar
1 cup (2 sticks) margarine or butter, softened
1/2 cup milk
1 teaspoon vanilla
1 teaspoon peppermint extract
1 egg
3 1/2 cups all-purpose flour
1 teaspoon baking powder
1/4 teaspoon salt
1/2 cup semisweet chocolate chips
1/2 cup chopped nuts
1/2 teaspoon red food color

Heat oven to 375°. Mix candies and 2 tablespoons sugar; reserve.

Mix sugar, margarine, milk, vanilla, peppermint extract and egg in large bowl. Stir in flour, baking powder and salt. Cover and refrigerate at least 4 hours.

Divide dough in half. Tint one half with food color. For each cookie, shape 1 teaspoon dough from each half into 4-inch rope on floured surface. Place one red and one white rope side by side; press together lightly and twist. Place on ungreased cookie sheet and curve one end of cookie to form handle of cane.

Bake 9 to 12 minutes or until set and very light brown. Immediately sprinkle reserved sugar mixture over cookies. Remove from cookie sheet. Cool on wire rack.

Serving Size: **1 Cookie** Calories 95 (Calories from Fat 45); Fat 5 g (Saturated 1 g); Cholesterol 5 mg; Sodium 60 mg; Carbohydrate 12 g; (Dietary Fiber 0 g); Protein 1 g

Santa Claus Cookies

About 1 1/2 dozen cookies

1 cup granulated sugar
1/2 cup shortening
2 tablespoons milk
1 teaspoon grated lemon peel
1 egg
2 cups all-purpose flour
1 teaspoon baking powder
1/2 teaspoon baking soda
1/2 teaspoon salt
Creamy Frosting (below) or Chocolate
   Frosting (right)
Red sugar
Miniature marshmallows
Currants or semisweet chocolate chips
Red cinnamon candies
Shredded coconut

Heat oven to 400°. Mix granulated sugar, shortening, milk, lemon peel and egg in large bowl. Stir in flour, baking powder, baking soda and salt. Shape dough into 1 1/4-inch balls. Place about 2 inches apart on ungreased cookie sheet. Flatten to about 2 1/2 inches in diameter with greased bottom of glass dipped in granulated sugar. Bake 8 to 10 minutes or until edges are light brown. Remove from cookie sheet. Cool on wire rack.

Spread 1 cookie with small amount of Creamy Frosting. (Frost and decorate cookies one at a time.) Sprinkle top third of cookie with red sugar for the hat. Press on miniature marshmallow for the tassel. Press 2 currants for the eyes and 1 red cinnamon candy for the nose into center third of cookie. Sprinkle coconut over bottom third for the beard.

Creamy Frosting

1 1/2 cups powdered sugar
1/2 teaspoon vanilla
2 to 3 tablespoons water

Mix all ingredients until spreading consistency.

Chocolate Frosting

2 ounces unsweetened chocolate
2 tablespoons margarine or butter
3 tablespoons water
About 2 cups powdered sugar

Heat chocolate and margarine in 1 1/2-quart saucepan over low heat, stirring until melted; remove from heat. Stir in water and powdered sugar until smooth and of spreading consistency.

Serving Size: 1 Cookie Calories 215 (Calories from Fat 65); Fat 7 g (Saturated 2 g); Cholesterol 10 mg; Sodium 130 mg; Carbohydrate 37 g; (Dietary Fiber 1 g); Protein 2 g

Christmas Bells

About 4 1/2 dozen cookies

1/2 cup sugar
1/4 cup (1/2 stick) margarine or butter, softened
1/4 cup shortening
1 egg
1 teaspoon vanilla
1 1/2 cups all-purpose flour
1/2 teaspoon salt
1/4 teaspoon baking soda
Red or green food color

Mix sugar, margarine, shortening, egg and vanilla. Stir in flour, salt and baking soda. Stir food color into two-thirds of the dough. Shape into roll, 10 × 1 1/2 inches. Form bell shape by pressing top of roll together and leaving lower half flared and curved. Wrap and refrigerate at least 1 hour.

Reserve 1/4 cup of the plain dough for clappers. Roll remaining plain dough into rectangle, about 10 × 5 inches, on waxed paper. Wrap around bell-shaped roll. Wrap and refrigerate at least 8 hours.

Heat oven to 375°. Cut roll into 1/8-inch slices. Place on ungreased cookie sheet. Place tiny ball of reserved dough at bottom of each bell for clapper. Bake until edges begin to brown, 7 to 8 minutes.

Serving Size: 1 Cookie Calories 40 (Calories from Fat 20); Fat 2 g (Saturated 0 g); Cholesterol 5 mg; Sodium 35 mg; Carbohydrate 5 g; (Dietary Fiber 0 g); Protein 0 g

Cherry Blinks

About 3 dozen cookies

1/2 cup sugar
1/3 cup shortening
1 tablespoon plus 1 1/2 teaspoons milk
1 teaspoon vanilla
1 egg
1 cup all-purpose flour
1/2 teaspoon baking powder
1/4 teaspoon baking soda
1/4 teaspoon salt
1/2 cup raisins
1/2 cup chopped nuts
1 3/4 cups whole wheat flake cereal, crushed
Candied or maraschino cherries

Heat oven to 375°. Mix sugar, shortening, milk, vanilla and egg. Stir in flour, baking powder, baking soda and salt. Stir in raisins and nuts. Drop dough by teaspoonfuls into crushed wheat flakes; roll gently until completely coated. Place cookies about 2 inches apart on ungreased cookie sheet. Press a cherry into each cookie. Bake until just set, 10 to 12 minutes. Remove from cookie sheet immediately.

Serving Size: 1 Cookie Calories 70 (Calories from Fat 25); Fat 3 g (Saturated 1 g); Cholesterol 5 mg; Sodium 50 mg; Carbohydrate 10 g; (Dietary Fiber 0 g); Protein 1 g

Russian Teacakes

About 4 dozen cookies

1 cup (2 sticks) margarine or butter, softened
1/2 cup powdered sugar
1 teaspoon vanilla
2 1/2 cups all-purpose flour
3/4 cup finely chopped nuts
1/4 teaspoon salt
Powdered sugar

Heat oven to 400°. Mix margarine, 1/2 cup powdered sugar and the vanilla. Stir in flour, nuts and salt until dough holds together. Shape into 1-inch balls. Place about 1 inch apart on

ungreased cookie sheet. Bake 10 to 12 minutes or until set but not brown.

Roll in powdered sugar while warm; cool. Roll in powdered sugar again.

Serving Size: 1 Cookie Calories 85 (Calories from Fat 45); Fat 5 g (Saturated 1 g); Cholesterol 0 mg; Sodium 55 mg; Carbohydrate 9 g; (Dietary Fiber 0 g); Protein 1 g

Berliner Kranzer

About 6 dozen cookies

We have made these German wreath-shaped cookies a bit easier than the traditional shaping method, to speed your holiday baking.

1 cup sugar
3/4 cup (1 1/2 sticks) margarine or butter, softened
3/4 cup shortening
2 teaspoons grated orange peel
2 eggs
4 cups all-purpose flour
1 egg white
2 tablespoons sugar
Red candied cherries
Green candied citron

Heat oven to 400°. Mix 1 cup sugar, the margarine, shortening, orange peel and eggs in large bowl. Mix in flour. Shape dough by rounded teaspoonfuls into ropes, 6 inches long. Form each rope into a circle, crossing ends and tucking under. (This shaping method is easier than the traditional method of tying knots.) Place on ungreased cookie sheet.

Beat egg white and 2 tablespoons sugar until foamy; brush over tops of cookies. Press bits of red candied cherries on center of knot for holly berries. Add "leaves" cut from green candied citron. Bake 10 to 12 minutes or until set but not brown. Immediately remove from cookie sheet. Cool on wire rack.

Serving Size: 1 Cookie Calories 80 (Calories from Fat 35); Fat 4 g (Saturated 1 g); Cholesterol 5 mg; Sodium 30 mg; Carbohydrate 10 g; (Dietary Fiber 0 g); Protein 1 g

Lebkuchen

About 5 dozen cookies

This cake-like cookie comes from Germany and is especially popular in Nuremberg. They are often baked in decorative molds, but our version is faster and just as tasty.

    1/2 cup honey
    1/2 cup molasses
    3/4 cup packed brown sugar
    1 teaspoon grated lemon peel
    1 tablespoon lemon juice
    1 egg
    2 3/4 cups all-purpose flour
    1 teaspoon ground allspice
    1 teaspoon ground cinnamon
    1 teaspoon ground cloves
    1 teaspoon ground nutmeg
    1/2 teaspoon baking soda
    1/3 cup chopped citron
    1/3 cup chopped nuts
    Cookie Glaze (below)

Mix honey and molasses in 3-quart saucepan. Heat to boiling, stirring occasionally; remove from heat. Cool completely. Stir in brown sugar, lemon peel, lemon juice and egg. Stir in flour, allspice, cinnamon, cloves, nutmeg and baking soda. Stir in citron and nuts. Cover and refrigerate at least 8 hours.

Heat oven to 400°. Grease cookie sheet. Roll about one-fourth of the dough at a time 1/4 inch thick on a lightly floured surface (keep remaining dough refrigerated). Cut dough into rectangles, 2 1/2 × 1 1/2 inches. Place 1 inch apart on cookie sheet. Bake 10 to 12 minutes or until no indentation remains when touched lightly. Immediately remove from cookie sheet. Cool on wire rack. Brush Cookie Glaze over cookies.

COOKIE GLAZE

    1 cup granulated sugar
    1/2 cup water
    1/4 cup powdered sugar

Mix granulated sugar and water in 1-quart saucepan. Cook over medium heat to 230° on candy thermometer or just until small amount of mixture spins a 2-inch thread when dropped from a spoon; remove from heat. Stir in powdered sugar. (If glaze becomes sugary while brushing cookies, heat slightly, adding a little water, until clear again.)

Serving Size: 1 Cookie Calories 75 (Calories from Fat 10); Fat 1 g (Saturated 0 g); Cholesterol 5 mg; Sodium 15 mg; Carbohydrate 16 g; (Dietary Fiber 0 g); Protein 1 g

Spritz

About 5 dozen cookies

Spritz are festive holiday cookies made with a special cookie press, available in most kitchenware stores. Top with currants, raisins, candies or slices of candied fruit before baking. After baking, decorate with colored sugar, nonpareils or red candies.

    1 cup (2 sticks) margarine or butter, softened
    1/2 cup sugar
    2 1/4 cups all-purpose flour
    1 teaspoon almond extract or vanilla
    1/2 teaspoon salt
    1 egg
    Few drops food color, if desired

Heat oven to 400°. Mix margarine and sugar in medium bowl. Stir in remaining ingredients. Place dough in cookie press. Form desired shapes on ungreased cookie sheet. Bake 6 to 9 minutes or until set but not brown. Remove from cookie sheet. Cool on wire rack.

CHOCOLATE SPRITZ: Stir 2 ounces unsweetened chocolate, melted and cooled, into margarine-sugar mixture. Omit food color.

Serving Size: 1 Cookie Calories 50 (Calories from Fat 25); Fat 3 g (Saturated 1 g); Cholesterol 5 mg; Sodium 55 mg; Carbohydrate 5 g; (Dietary Fiber 0 g); Protein 1 g

Almond-filled Crescents

4 dozen cookies

1 cup powdered sugar
1 cup whipping (heavy) cream
2 eggs
3 3/4 cups all-purpose flour
1 teaspoon baking powder
1/2 teaspoon salt
1 package (about 8 ounces) almond paste
3/4 cup (1 1/2 sticks) margarine or butter, softened
Glaze (below)

Mix powdered sugar, whipping cream and eggs in large bowl. Stir in flour, baking powder and salt. (Dough will be stiff.) Cover and refrigerate about 1 hour or until firm.

Heat oven to 375°. Break almond paste into small pieces in medium bowl; add margarine. Beat on low speed until blended. Beat on high speed until fluffy (tiny bits of almond paste will remain).

Roll one-fourth of the dough at a time into 10-inch circle on lightly floured surface. Spread one-fourth of almond paste mixture (about 1/2 cup) over circle. Cut into 12 wedges. Roll up, beginning at rounded edge. Place on ungreased cookie sheet with points underneath. Curve cookies to form crescents. Repeat with remaining dough and almond paste mixture. Bake 14 to 16 minutes or until golden brown. Remove from cookie sheet. Cool completely on wire rack. Drizzle Glaze over crescents.

GLAZE

1 cup powdered sugar
6 to 7 teaspoons milk

Mix ingredients until smooth and of drizzling consistency.

Serving Size: 1 Cookie Calories 120 (Calories from Fat 55); Fat 6 g (Saturated 2 g); Cholesterol 15 mg; Sodium 70 mg; Carbohydrate 15 g; (Dietary Fiber 0 g); Protein 2 g

Hamantaschen

About 4 1/2 dozen cookies

1 cup sugar
1/3 cup vegetable oil
3 eggs
Grated peel and juice from 1 orange
3 1/4 cups all-purpose flour
2 teaspoons baking powder
1/2 teaspoon salt
Filling (below)

Beat sugar, oil and eggs until blended. Stir in orange peel and orange juice. Mix in flour, baking powder and salt. Cover and refrigerate at least 2 hours.

Heat oven to 375°. Divide dough into halves. Roll each half 1/8 inch thick on lightly floured, cloth-covered board. Cut into 3-inch rounds. Spoon 1 teaspoon Filling onto each round. Fold each round to form triangle. Pinch edges together to form slight ridge. Place on lightly greased cookie sheet. Bake until golden brown, 12 to 15 minutes.

FILLING

1 pound cut-up cooked prunes
1 cup chopped nuts
1 tablespoon sugar
1 tablespoon lemon juice

Mix all ingredients.

Serving Size: 1 Cookie Calories 80 (Calories from Fat 25); Fat 3 g (Saturated 0 g); Cholesterol 10 mg; Sodium 40 mg; Carbohydrate 13 g; (Dietary Fiber 1 g); Protein 1 g

Valentine's Day Cookies/Chocolate Linzer Hearts

Valentine's Day Cookies

About 4 dozen cookies

1 cup powdered sugar
1 cup (2 sticks) margarine or butter, softened
1 tablespoon vinegar
2 1/4 cups all-purpose flour
1 1/2 teaspoons ground ginger
3/4 teaspoon baking soda
1/4 teaspoon salt
6 drops red food color

Heat oven to 400°. Mix powdered sugar, margarine and vinegar in large bowl. Stir in remaining ingredients except food color. Divide dough in half. Mix food color into one half. (If dough is too dry, work in milk, 1 teaspoon at a time.) Roll dough 1/8 inch thick on lightly floured, cloth-covered surface. Cut into various size heart shapes with cookie cutters. Mix and match sizes and colors. Place about 2 inches apart on ungreased cookie sheet. Bake 5 to 7 minutes or until set but not brown. Cool slightly. Carefully remove from cookie sheet. Cool completely. Decorate with white and pink Decorator's Frosting (p.10), if desired.

Serving Size: 1 Cookie Calories 70 (Calories from Fat 35); Fat 4 g (Saturated 1 g); Cholesterol 0 mg; Sodium 75 mg; Carbohydrate 7 g; (Dietary Fiber 0 g); Protein 1 g

Chocolate Linzer Hearts

3 dozen sandwich cookies

1 cup (2 sticks) margarine or butter, softened
1/2 cup sugar
2 eggs
1 teaspoon vanilla
2 1/2 cups all-purpose flour
1 cup hazelnuts, toasted, skinned and ground
1 1/2 teaspoons ground cinnamon
1/2 teaspoon ground nutmeg
1/2 ounce semisweet chocolate, finely chopped
1/2 cup raspberry jam
1 ounce semisweet chocolate, melted

Beat margarine and sugar in large bowl until light and fluffy. Beat in eggs and vanilla until smooth. Add remaining ingredients except jam and melted chocolate. Beat until well blended. Cover and refrigerate dough 1 hour. (Dough will be sticky.)

Heat oven to 375°. Roll one-fourth of dough at a time 1/8 inch thick on lightly floured surface. (Keep remaining dough refrigerated until ready to roll.)

Cut with 2-inch heart-shaped cookie cutter. Cut out centers of half the cookies, if desired. Place on ungreased cookie sheet. Bake 7 to 9 minutes or until light brown. Remove from cookie sheet. Cool completely. Put cookies together in pairs with about 1/2 teaspoon raspberry jam each. Drizzle with melted chocolate.

Serving Size: 1 Cookie Calories 125 (Calories from Fat 65); Fat 7 g (Saturated 1 g); Cholesterol 10 mg; Sodium 65 mg; Carbohydrate 14 g; (Dietary Fiber 0 g); Protein 2 g

Witches' Hats

32 hats

No tricks! These treats are super simple to throw together if you need something in a snap for a party or any unexpected ghosts or goblins.

32 foil-wrapped milk chocolate kisses, unwrapped
1 package (11 1/2 ounces) fudge-striped shortbread cookies (32 cookies)
1 tube (4.25 ounces) orange or red decorating icing

Attach chocolate kiss to chocolate bottom of each cookie with decorating icing. Pipe decorating icing around base of chocolate kiss.

Serving Size: 1 Cookie Calories 90 (Calories from Fat 35); Fat 4 g (Saturated 2 g); Cholesterol 2 mg; Sodium 35 mg; Carbohydrate 12 g; (Dietary Fiber 0 g); Protein 1 g

Cookie Exchange

Send out invitations three weeks in advance so everyone has time to prepare one dozen cookies for each of the guests. Let participants know what other guests are planning to bring so cookies aren't duplicated.

Ask each guest to bring the cookies arranged on sturdy plastic or paper plates covered with plastic wrap or in plastic bags or other containers. Ask guests to label their cookies and provide any special storage instructions.

If recipes also will be exchanged, ask for the recipes before the cookie exchange so there is time to make copies for all the guests.

Witches' Brooms

20 brooms

1/2 cup packed brown sugar
1/2 cup (1 stick) margarine or butter, softened
2 tablespoons water
1 teaspoon vanilla
1 1/2 cups all-purpose flour
1/8 teaspoon salt
10 pretzel rods (about 8 1/2 inches long), cut crosswise in half
2 teaspoons shortening
2/3 cup semisweet chocolate chips
1/3 cup butterscotch flavored chips

Heat oven to 350°. Mix brown sugar, margarine, water and vanilla in medium bowl. Stir in flour and salt. Shape dough into twenty 1 1/4-inch balls.

Place pretzel rod halves on ungreased cookie sheet. Press ball of dough onto cut end of each pretzel rod. Press dough with fork to resemble "bristles" of broom. Bake about 12 minutes or until set but not brown. Remove from cookie sheet. Cool completely on wire rack.

Cover cookie sheet with waxed paper. Place brooms on waxed paper. Heat shortening and chocolate chips over low heat, stirring occasionally, until melted and smooth; remove from heat. Spoon melted chocolate over brooms, leaving about 3 inches at top of pretzel handle and bottom halves of cookie bristles uncovered. Place butterscotch chips in microwavable bowl. Microwave uncovered on Medium-high (70%) 30 to 50 seconds, stirring after 30 seconds, until chips can be stirred smooth. Microwave additional 10 to 20 seconds, stirring until smooth. Drizzle over chocolate. Let stand until chocolate is set.

Serving Size: 1 Cookie Calories 170 (Calories from Fat 70); Fat 8 g (Saturated 3 g); Cholesterol 0 mg; Sodium 190 mg; Carbohydrate 24 g; (Dietary Fiber 1 g); Protein 2 g

Witches' Brooms, Witches' Hats

Magic Window Cookies

About 6 dozen 3-inch cookies

1 cup sugar
3/4 cup (1 1/2 sticks) margarine or butter,
    softened
1 teaspoon vanilla or 1/2 teaspoon lemon extract
2 eggs
2 1/2 cups all-purpose flour
1 teaspoon baking powder
1/4 teaspoon salt
4 rolls (about 0.9 ounces each) ring-shaped hard
    candy

Mix sugar, margarine, vanilla and eggs in large
bowl. Stir in flour, baking powder and salt. Cover
and refrigerate about 1 hour or until firm.

Heat oven to 375°. Cover cookie sheet with aluminum foil. Roll one-third of dough at a time
1/8 inch thick on lightly floured, cloth-covered
board. Cut into desired Halloween shapes with
cookie cutters. Place on foil. Cut out designs from
cookies using smaller cutters or your own patterns. Place whole or partially crushed pieces of
candy in cutouts, depending on size and shape of
design, mixing colors as desired. (To crush candy,
place in heavy plastic bag and tap lightly with
rolling pin. Because candy melts easily, leave
pieces as large as possible.)

Bake 7 to 9 minutes or until cookies are very light
brown and candy is melted. If candy has not completely spread within cutout design, immediately
spread with knife. Cool completely on foil.
Remove cookies gently.

Serving Size: 1 Cookie Calories 55 (Calories from Fat 20);
Fat 2 g (Saturated 0 g); Cholesterol 5 mg; Sodium
40 mg; Carbohydrate 8 g; (Dietary Fiber 0 g); Protein 1 g

Candy Corn Shortbread

About 3 dozen cookies

3/4 cup (1 1/2 sticks) margarine or butter,
    softened
1/4 cup sugar
2 cups all-purpose flour
Yellow food color
Red food color

Mix margarine and sugar in large bowl. Stir in
flour. Divide dough into 6 equal parts. Combine
3 parts dough; mix with 10 drops yellow and
4 drops red food color (for orange dough).
Combine 2 parts dough; mix with 7 drops yellow
food color (for yellow dough). Leave remaining
part dough plain.

Pat orange dough into 3/4-inch-thick rectangle,
9 × 2 inches, on plastic wrap. Pat yellow dough
into 1/2-inch-thick rectangle, 9 × 1 3/4 inches.
Place yellow rectangle lengthwise in center on top
of orange rectangle. Roll plain dough into roll,
9 × 3/4 inch. Place lengthwise in center on top of
yellow rectangle. Wrap plastic wrap around
dough, pressing dough into triangle so that dough
will resemble a kernel of corn when sliced.
Refrigerate about 2 hours or until firm.

Heat oven to 350°. Cut dough into 1/4-inch
slices. Place about 1 inch apart on ungreased
cookie sheet. Bake 10 to 12 minutes or until set.
Remove from cookie sheet. Cool on wire rack.

*Stack dough so that the
orange rectangle is on the
bottom and the uncolored
roll of dough is on top.*

*Press dough into triangle so
that sliced wedges resemble
a kernel of corn.*

Serving Size: 1 Cookie Calories 70 (Calories from Fat 35);
Fat 4 g (Saturated 1 g); Cholesterol 0 mg; Sodium
45 mg; Carbohydrate 7 g; (Dietary Fiber 0 g); Protein 1 g

Candy Corn Shortbread/Magic Window Cookies

Glazed Cranberry Cookies

About 5 1/2 dozen cookies

1 cup granulated sugar
3/4 cup packed brown sugar
1/2 cup (1 stick) margarine or butter, softened
1/4 cup milk
2 tablespoons orange juice
1 egg
3 cups all-purpose flour
1 teaspoon baking powder
1/2 teaspoon salt
1/4 teaspoon baking soda
2 1/2 cups coarsely chopped cranberries
1 cup chopped nuts
Browned Butter Glaze (below)

Heat oven to 375°. Mix sugars and margarine. Stir in milk, orange juice and egg. Stir in remaining ingredients except Browned Butter Glaze. Drop by rounded teaspoonfuls about 2 inches apart onto greased cookie sheet. Bake until light brown, 10 to 15 minutes. Cool; spread with glaze, if desired.

BROWNED BUTTER GLAZE

1/3 cup margarine or butter
2 cups powdered sugar
1 1/2 teaspoons vanilla
2 to 4 tablespoons hot water

Heat margarine over low heat until golden brown; cool slightly. Stir in powdered sugar and vanilla. Beat in hot water until smooth and of desired consistency.

Serving Size: 1 Cookie Calories 110 (Calories from Fat 35); Fat 4 g (Saturated 1 g); Cholesterol 5 mg; Sodium 60 mg; Carbohydrate 17 g; (Dietary Fiber 0 g); Protein 1 g

Applesauce-Spice Drops

About 7 dozen cookies

2 cups packed brown sugar
1 cup shortening
1/2 cup cold coffee
2 cups applesauce
2 eggs
3 1/2 cups all-purpose flour
1 teaspoon baking soda
1 teaspoon salt
1 teaspoon ground cinnamon
1 teaspoon ground nutmeg
1 teaspoon ground cloves
1 cup raisins
1/2 cup coarsely chopped nuts

Heat oven to 400°. Mix brown sugar, shortening, coffee, applesauce and eggs. Stir in remaining ingredients (dough will be very soft). Drop by rounded teaspoonfuls about 2 inches apart onto lightly greased cookie sheet. Bake until almost no indentation remains when touched, about 7 minutes.

Serving Size: 1 Cookie Calories 80 (Calories from Fat 25); Fat 3 g (Saturated 1 g); Cholesterol 5 mg; Sodium 45 mg; Carbohydrate 12 g; (Dietary Fiber 0 g); Protein 1 g

Frosted Pumpkin-Pecan Cookies

About 5 dozen cookies

Soft and cinnamon-kissed, these pumpkin cookies celebrate the plenty of harvest time.

1 1/2 cups packed brown sugar
1/2 cup (1 stick) margarine or butter, softened
1/2 cup shortening
1 cup canned pumpkin
1 egg
2 1/3 cups all-purpose flour
1 teaspoon baking powder
1/2 teaspoon salt
1/2 teaspoon ground cinnamon
2 cups chopped pecans
Frosting (right)

Heat oven to 350°. Mix brown sugar, margarine and shortening in large bowl. Stir in pumpkin and egg. Stir in flour, baking powder, salt and cinnamon. Stir in pecans.

Drop by rounded tablespoonfuls about 2 inches apart onto ungreased cookie sheet; flatten slightly. Bake 12 to 15 minutes or until no indentation remains when touched lightly in center. Remove from cookie sheet. Cool completely. Prepare Frosting and spread each cookie with about 1 teaspoon.

FROSTING

3 cups powdered sugar
1/4 cup (1/2 stick) margarine or butter, softened
3 to 4 tablespoons milk
1/4 teaspoon ground cinnamon

Mix all ingredients until smooth and of desired consistency.

Serving Size: 1 Cookie Calories 130 (Calories from Fat 65); Fat 7 g (Saturated 1 g); Cholesterol 5 mg; Sodium 55 mg; Carbohydrate 16 g; (Dietary Fiber 0 g); Protein 1 g

Cranberry-Orange Cookies

About 4 dozen cookies

Cranberries are harvested in the autumn, but can be found year 'round in supermarkets. With all the lovely flavors of a holiday cranberry quickbread, these cookies are soft-centered with slightly crunchy edges.

1 cup granulated sugar
1/2 cup packed brown sugar
1 cup (2 sticks) margarine or butter, softened
1 teaspoon grated orange peel
2 tablespoons orange juice
1 egg
2 1/2 cups all-purpose flour
2 cups coarsely chopped cranberries
1/2 cup chopped nuts, if desired
1/2 teaspoon baking soda
1/2 teaspoon salt
Orange Glaze (below)

Heat oven to 375°. Mix sugars, margarine, orange peel, orange juice and egg in large bowl. Stir in remaining ingredients except Orange Glaze.

Drop by rounded tablespoonfuls about 2 inches apart onto ungreased cookie sheet. Bake 12 to 14 minutes or until light brown. Remove from cookie sheet. Cool completely. Prepare Orange Glaze and spread each cookie with about 1/2 teaspoon.

ORANGE GLAZE

1 1/2 cups powdered sugar
3 tablespoons orange juice
1/2 teaspoon grated orange peel

Mix all ingredients until smooth.

Serving Size: 1 Cookie Calories 105 (Calories from Fat 35); Fat 4 g (Saturated 1 g); Cholesterol 5 mg; Sodium 80 mg; Carbohydrate 16 g; (Dietary Fiber 0 g); Protein 1 g

Cookie Pizza

6

Cookies for Kids

Cookie Pizza

16 servings

If you like, try spelling out special messages with the chocolate candies to personalize your cookie.

1/2 cup packed brown sugar
1/4 cup granulated sugar
1/2 cup (1 stick) margarine or butter, softened
1 teaspoon vanilla
1 egg
1 1/4 cups all-purpose flour
1/2 teaspoon baking soda
1 package (6 ounces) miniature semisweet chocolate chips
1 cup sweetened whipped cream
1/4 cup chopped walnuts
1/4 cup flaked or shredded coconut, toasted
1/2 cup candy-coated chocolate candies

Heat oven to 350°. Mix sugars, margarine, vanilla and egg. Stir in flour and baking soda (dough will be stiff). Stir in chocolate chips. Spread or pat dough in ungreased 12-inch pizza pan or on cookie sheet. Bake about 15 minutes or until golden brown; cool. Just before serving, spread cookie with whipped cream. Sprinkle with walnuts, coconut and chocolate candies. Cut into wedges. Refrigerate any remaining cookie.

Serving Size: 1 Serving Calories 255 (Calories from Fat 125); Fat 14 g (Saturated 6 g); Cholesterol 20 mg; Sodium 130 mg; Carbohydrate 30 g; (Dietary Fiber 1 g); Protein 3 g

Peanut Butter Lollipop Cookies

2 to 2 1/2 dozen cookies

Children find these cookies enchanting. Decorate them any way you like, with faces, names or abstract designs.

1/2 cup granulated sugar
1/2 cup packed brown sugar
1/2 cup creamy peanut butter
1/2 cup (1 stick) margarine or butter, softened
1/4 cup shortening
1 egg
1 2/3 cups all-purpose flour
3/4 teaspoon baking soda
1/2 teaspoon baking powder
1/4 teaspoon salt
25 to 30 wooden ice cream or lollipop sticks
Glaze (below)
Chocolate sprinkles
Decorator Frosting (right)

Mix sugars, peanut butter, margarine, shortening and egg in large bowl. Stir in flour, baking soda, baking powder and salt. Cover and refrigerate about 1 hour or until firm.

Heat oven to 375°. Roll half of dough at a time 1/8 inch thick on floured, cloth-covered surface with cloth-covered rolling pin. Cut into 2 1/2-inch rounds. Place about 3 inches apart on ungreased cookie sheet. Lightly press to seal. Bake 10 to 11 minutes or until light brown. Cool slightly; remove from cookie sheet. Cool completely.

Prepare Glaze and spread evenly on top of one cookie at a time. Immediately coat edge with chocolate sprinkles. Repeat with remaining cookies. Prepare Decorator Frosting and place in decorating bag with #3 or #4 writing tip and decorate cookies.

GLAZE

2 cups powdered sugar
2 tablespoons water
2 tablespoons light corn syrup

Mix all ingredients in saucepan until smooth. Heat over low heat just until lukewarm (1 to 2 minutes); remove from heat. If necessary, add hot water, a few drops at a time, until of spreading consistency.

DECORATOR FROSTING

1 cup powdered sugar
1 tablespoon creamy peanut butter
3 to 4 teaspoons milk
1/2 teaspoon cocoa

Mix all ingredients until smooth and of piping consistency.

Serving Size: 1 Cookie Calories 235 (Calories from Fat 90); Fat 10 g (Saturated 2 g); Cholesterol 10 mg; Sodium 150 mg; Carbohydrate 34 g; (Dietary Fiber 1 g); Protein 3 g

Candy Cookies

About 3 dozen cookies

1/2 cup granulated sugar
1/2 cup packed brown sugar
1/3 cup margarine or butter, softened
1/3 cup shortening
1 teaspoon vanilla
1 egg
1 1/2 cups all-purpose flour
1/2 teaspoon baking soda
1/2 teaspoon salt
1 package (8 ounces) chocolate-coated candies

Heat oven to 375°. Mix sugars, margarine, shortening, vanilla and egg. Stir in remaining ingredients. Drop dough by heaping teaspoonfuls about 2 inches apart onto ungreased cookie sheet. Bake until light brown, 8 to 10 minutes. (Centers will be soft.) Cool slightly; remove from cookie sheet.

Serving Size: 1 Cookie Calories 105 (Calories from Fat 45); Fat 5 g (Saturated 2 g); Cholesterol 5 mg; Sodium 75 mg; Carbohydrate 14 g; (Dietary Fiber 0 g); Protein 1 g

Peanut Butter Lollipop Cookies, Chocolate Peanut Windmills (p.72)

Thumbprint Cookies

About 3 dozen cookies

1/4 cup packed brown sugar
1/4 cup shortening
1/4 cup (1/2 stick) margarine or butter, softened
1/2 teaspoon vanilla
1 egg, separated
1 cup all-purpose flour
1/4 teaspoon salt
1 cup finely chopped nuts
Jelly

Heat oven to 350°. Mix brown sugar, shortening, margarine, vanilla and egg yolk. Stir in flour and salt until dough holds together. Shape into 1-inch balls.

Beat egg white slightly. Dip each ball into egg white. Roll in nuts. Place about 1 inch apart on ungreased cookie sheet. Press thumb deeply in center of each. Bake about 10 minutes or until light brown; cool. Fill thumbprints with jelly.

Serving Size: 1 Cookie Calories 75 (Calories from Fat 45); Fat 5 g (Saturated 1 g); Cholesterol 5 mg; Sodium 35 mg; Carbohydrate 6 g; (Dietary Fiber 0 g); Protein 1 g

Chocolate-Peanut Windmills

About 2 dozen cookies

1 cup sugar
1/3 cup margarine or butter, softened
1/3 cup shortening
2 tablespoons milk
1/2 teaspoon vanilla
1 egg
2 ounces unsweetened chocolate, melted and cooled
1 3/4 cups all-purpose flour
1 teaspoon baking powder
1/8 teaspoon salt
1/2 cup finely chopped peanuts

Mix sugar, margarine, shortening, milk, vanilla and egg in large bowl. Stir in chocolate. Stir in flour, baking powder and salt. Cover and refrigerate about 2 hours or until firm.

Heat oven to 400°. Roll half the dough at a time into rectangle, 12 × 9 inches, on lightly floured, cloth-covered surface. Sprinkle each rectangle with half the peanuts. Gently press into dough. Cut dough into 3-inch squares. Place about 2 inches apart on ungreased cookie sheet. Cut squares diagonally from each corner almost to center. Fold every other point to center to resemble pinwheel. Bake about 6 minutes or until set. Cool 2 minutes; remove from cookie sheet.

 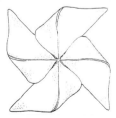

Cut squares diagonally from each corner almost to center.

Fold every other point to center to resemble pinwheel.

Serving Size: 1 Cookie Calories 145 (Calories from Fat 70); Fat 8 g (Saturated 2 g); Cholesterol 10 mg; Sodium 65 mg; Carbohydrate 17 g; (Dietary Fiber 1 g); Protein 2 g

Bear Claws

About 1 1/2 dozen cookies

1/2 cup granulated sugar
1/4 cup (1/2 stick) margarine or butter, softened
2 tablespoons shortening
1 egg
1 teaspoon vanilla
1 1/4 cups all-purpose flour
1/2 teaspoon baking powder
1/2 teaspoon salt
About 3 tablespoons raspberry jam
About 3 tablespoons chopped nuts
About 3 tablespoons powdered sugar

Mix granulated sugar, margarine, shortening, egg and vanilla. Stir in flour, baking powder and salt. Cover and refrigerate at least 1 hour.

Heat oven to 400°. Roll dough into 12-inch square on lightly floured, cloth-covered board. Cut into 3-inch squares. Spread about 1/2 teaspoon jam down center of each square; sprinkle with about 1/2 teaspoon nuts. Fold 1 edge of dough over filling; fold other edge over top. Place on greased cookie sheet. Make 4 or 5 cuts in 1 long side of each cookie; spread cuts slightly apart. Sprinkle each cookie with about 1/2 teaspoon powdered sugar. Bake until light brown, about 6 minutes.

Serving Size: 1 Cookie Calories 115 (Calories from Fat 45); Fat 5 g (Saturated 1 g); Cholesterol 10 mg; Sodium 110 mg; Carbohydrate 16 g; (Dietary Fiber 0 g); Protein 1 g

Mailing Cookie Care Packages

Gifts of homemade cookies sent to hardworking college students, busy young families or out-of-town grandparents are always welcome.

Choose sturdy cookies, such as Ultimate Chocolate Chip Cookies (page 14) or Hermits (page 22). Drop cookies or other hearty cookies in simple shapes are almost always good travelers.

Wrap cookies in pairs, back to back, and place them flat or on end in a can, box or other durable container.

Fill each container as full as practical, padding the top with crushed waxed paper to prevent shaking and breakage.

Pack containers in a corrugated or fiberboard packing box that's lined with aluminum foil. For fill, use crumpled newspaper, shredded paper or shredded polyethylene foam. Be sure to pack several inches of fill in the bottom of the packing box and in between items so the contents cannot move easily.

Seal package box with shipping tape, and cover the address label with transparent tape for protection. Label the package "Perishable" to encourage careful handling.

Cinnamon Footballs, Multigrain Cutouts

Cinnamon Footballs

About 2 dozen cookies

1/2 cup packed brown sugar
1/2 cup (1 stick) margarine or butter, softened
1 teaspoon vanilla
1 1/2 cups all-purpose flour
1/2 teaspoon ground cinnamon
1/8 teaspoon salt
About 24 whole blanched almonds
Decorating Glaze (below)

Heat oven to 350°. Mix brown sugar, margarine and vanilla in large bowl. Work in flour, cinnamon and salt until dough holds together. (If dough is dry, mix in 1 to 2 tablespoons milk.)

Shape dough by scant tablespoonfuls around almonds to form football shapes. Place about 1 inch apart on ungreased cookie sheet. Bake 12 to 14 minutes or until set but not brown. Remove from cookie sheet. Cool completely. Prepare Decorating Glaze and place in decorating bag with #3 writing tip. Make football laces on cookies.

Decorating Glaze

1/2 cup powdered sugar
1 1/2 to 3 teaspoons water

Mix powdered sugar and just enough water to make paste that can be piped from decorating bag.

CINNAMON-BASEBALLS: Substitute pitted dates, cut in half crosswise, for the almonds. Mold dough around date half into baseball shape. Pipe on laces.

Serving Size: 1 Cookie Calories 100 (Calories from Fat 45); Fat 5 g (Saturated 1 g); Cholesterol 0 mg; Sodium 60 mg; Carbohydrate 13 g; (Dietary Fiber 0 g); Protein 1 g

Multigrain Cutouts

About 6 dozen 2- to 3-inch cookies.

Perfect for a sports party, these hearty cookies have a nutty, not-too-sweet flavor. The "dump" method of mixing all the ingredients together makes these cookies supereasy.

3 1/4 cups whole wheat flour
1 cup sugar
2/3 cup shortening
1/4 cup cornmeal
1/4 cup wheat germ
3/4 cup milk
1 teaspoon baking powder
1/2 teaspoon salt
1/2 teaspoon vanilla
Baked-on Frosting (below)

Heat oven to 350°. Mix all ingredients except Baked-on Frosting.

Roll about one-third of dough at a time 1/8 inch thick on lightly floured surface. Cut with sport-shaped cookie cutters. Place on ungreased cookie sheet. Prepare Baked-on Frosting and place in decorating bag with #5 writing tip. Outline or decorate unbaked cookies. Bake 12 to 14 minutes or until edges are light brown. Cool slightly. Remove from cookie sheet.

Baked-on Frosting

2/3 cup all-purpose flour
2/3 cup margarine or butter, softened
1 tablespoon hot water

Mix flour and margarine until smooth. Stir in hot water.

Serving Size: 1 Cookie Calories 70 (Calories from Fat 35); Fat 4 g (Saturated 1 g); Cholesterol 0 mg; Sodium 45 mg; Carbohydrate 8 g; (Dietary Fiber 0 g); Protein 1 g

Cow Cookies

Cow Cookies

About 6 dozen cookies

1 cup sugar
1/4 cup shortening
1/4 cup (1/2 stick) margarine or butter, softened
1 teaspoon vanilla
1 egg
2 2/3 cups all-purpose flour
1/2 cup sour cream
1 teaspoon baking powder
1/2 teaspoon baking soda
1/2 teaspoon salt
1/4 teaspoon ground nutmeg
1 ounce unsweetened chocolate, melted and
   cooled
Pink Frosting (below)

Heat oven to 425°. Mix sugar, shortening, margarine, vanilla and the egg in medium bowl. Stir in remaining ingredients except chocolate and Pink Frosting. Divide dough into 3 equal parts. Mix chocolate into 1 part dough; divide chocolate dough into 2 equal parts.

Drop small portions of 1 part plain dough and 1 part chocolate dough close together in random pattern onto lightly floured cloth-covered surface. Roll plain and chocolate doughs together into marbled pattern to 1/8-inch thickness. (Press the portions of plain and chocolate doughs together to keep from separating while rolling.) Cut with 3-inch cow-shaped cookie cutter. Place on ungreased cookie sheet. Repeat with remaining plain and chocolate doughs.

Bake about 5 minutes or until no imprint remains when touched; cool. Decorate as desired with frosting.

PINK FROSTING

1 cup powdered sugar
1 drop red food color
About 3 teaspoons water

Mix all ingredients until spreading consistency.

Serving Size: 1 Cookie Calories 55 (Calories from Fat 20); Fat 2 g (Saturated 1 g); Cholesterol 5 mg; Sodium 40 mg; Carbohydrate 8 g; (Dietary Fiber 0 g); Protein 1 g

Snickerdoodles

About 6 dozen cookies.

These chewy cinnamon cookies were called Schneckerdoodles in the cookbooks of nineteenth-century German and Dutch settlers.

1 1/2 cups sugar
1/2 cup (1 stick) margarine or butter, softened
1/2 cup shortening
2 eggs
2 3/4 cups all-purpose flour
2 teaspoons cream of tartar
1 teaspoon baking soda
1/4 teaspoon salt
2 tablespoons sugar
2 teaspoons ground cinnamon

Heat oven to 400°. Mix 1 1/2 cups sugar, the margarine, shortening and eggs thoroughly in 3-quart bowl. Stir in flour, cream of tartar, baking soda and salt until blended. Shape dough by rounded teaspoonfuls into balls.

Mix 2 tablespoons sugar and the cinnamon; roll balls in sugar mixture. Place about 2 inches apart on ungreased cookie sheet. Bake until set, 8 to 10 minutes. Immediately remove from cookie sheet.

Serving Size: 1 Cookie Calories 65 (Calories from Fat 25); Fat 3 g (Saturated 1 g); Cholesterol 5 mg; Sodium 40 mg; Carbohydrate 8 g; (Dietary Fiber 0 g); Protein 1 g

Cream Cheese Cookie Tarts

24 tarts

1/2 cup margarine or butter, softened
1/3 cup sugar
3 tablespoons milk
1/4 teaspoon salt
1/4 teaspoon vanilla
2/3 cup whole wheat flour
2/3 cup all-purpose flour
1 package (8 ounces) cream cheese, softened
1/4 cup sugar
3 tablespoons all-purpose flour
1 egg yolk
Lemon Filling (below)
Chocolate Filling (below)
Flaked coconut
Chopped nuts

Mix margarine, 1/3 cup sugar, the milk, salt and vanilla in medium bowl. Stir in whole wheat flour and 2/3 cup all-purpose flour. Cover and refrigerate pastry 30 minutes.

Heat oven to 375°. Mix cream cheese, 1/4 cup sugar, 3 tablespoons all-purpose flour and the egg yolk; divide in half. Prepare Lemon Filling and Chocolate Filling. Press 1 tablespoon pastry onto bottom and 3/8 inch up side of each of 24 medium muffin cups, 2 1/2 × 1 1/4 inches. Spoon scant tablespoon Lemon Filling into 12 tarts; sprinkle with coconut. Spoon scant tablespoon Chocolate Filling into remaining 12 tarts; sprinkle with nuts. Bake 12 to 15 minutes or until pastry is light brown around edges. Cool slightly; remove from pan. Cool completely.

Lemon Filling

Stir in 1/4 teaspoon grated lemon peel and 1 teaspoon lemon juice into half of the cream cheese mixture.

Chocolate Filling

Stir 2 tablespoons sugar and 2 tablespoons cocoa into other half of the cream cheese mixture.

Serving Size: 1 Tart Calories 130 (Calories from Fat 70); Fat 8 g (Saturated 3 g); Cholesterol 20 mg; Sodium 100 mg; Carbohydrate 13 g; (Dietary Fiber 0 g); Protein 2 g

Peanut Butter Brownie Treats

12 brownies

Baked individually in muffin pans, these brownie treats are easy to take along on picnics or tuck into a lunch box.

2 cups (12 ounces) semisweet chocolate chips
1/4 cup (1/2 stick) margarine or butter
1/2 cup peanut butter
3 eggs
1 teaspoon vanilla
1 1/2 cups sugar
1 1/4 cups all-purpose flour
1/2 teaspoon baking powder
Peanut Butter Frosting (below)

Heat oven to 350°. Grease bottoms only of 12 medium muffin cups, 2 1/2 × 1 1/4 inches, or line with paper baking cups. Melt chocolate chips and margarine in 2-quart saucepan over low heat. Stir in peanut butter until well blended. Beat in eggs, one at a time, until smooth; stir in vanilla. Beat in remaining ingredients except frosting until smooth. Divide batter evenly among muffin cups. Bake 18 to 22 minutes or until tops are dry. Cool; spread with frosting. Decorate each with a miniature peanut butter cup, if desired.

Peanut Butter Frosting

1 1/2 cups powdered sugar
2 tablespoons peanut butter
1/2 teaspoon vanilla
2 tablespoons milk

Mix all ingredients until smooth.

Serving Size: 1 Brownie Calories 475 (Calories from Fat 180); Fat 20 g (Saturated 7 g); Cholesterol 55 mg; Sodium 150 mg; Carbohydrate 71 g; (Dietary Fiber 4 g); Protein 7 g

Confetti Caramel Bars

3 dozen bars

You choose the topping! Another popular combination we tested was candy corn, candy-coated chocolate candies and salted peanuts.

    1 cup packed brown sugar
    1 cup (2 sticks) margarine or butter, softened
    1 1/2 teaspoons vanilla
    1 egg
    2 cups all-purpose flour
    1/2 cup light corn syrup
    2 tablespoons margarine or butter
    1 cup (6 ounces) butterscotch flavored chips
    1 1/2 to 2 cups assorted candies and nuts (such as
        colored chocolate chips, candy corn, candy-
        coated chocolate candies and salted peanuts)

Heat oven to 350°. Mix brown sugar, 1 cup margarine, the vanilla and egg in large bowl. Stir in flour. Spread evenly in bottom of ungreased rectangular pan, 13 × 9 × 2 inches. Bake 20 to 22 minutes or until light brown. Cool 20 minutes.

Heat corn syrup, 2 tablespoons margarine and the butterscotch chips in heavy 1-quart saucepan over low heat, stirring constantly, until chips are melted; remove from heat. Cool 10 minutes.

Spread butterscotch mixture over baked layer. Sprinkle with candy and nuts; gently press into butterscotch mixture. Cover and refrigerate at least 2 hours until butterscotch mixture is firm. Cut into 2 × 1 1/2-inch bars.

Serving Size: 1 Bar Calories 165 (Calories from Fat 70); Fat 8 g (Saturated 3 g); Cholesterol 5 mg; Sodium 90 mg; Carbohydrate 21 g; (Dietary Fiber 0 g); Protein 2 g

Nutty Marshmallow Bars

24 bars

    1 cup chopped salted blanched peanuts
    3/4 cup all-purpose flour
    3/4 cup quick-cooking or regular oats
    2/3 cup packed brown sugar
    1/2 teaspoon baking soda
    1/2 teaspoon salt
    1 egg
    1/3 cup margarine or butter, softened
    1 jar (7 ounces) marshmallow creme
    1/3 cup caramel ice-cream topping
    1 cup salted blanched peanuts

Heat oven to 350°. Stir choped peanuts, flour, oats, brown sugar, baking soda, salt and egg in large bowl. Stir in margarine until mixture is crumbly.

Press in ungreased rectangular pan, 13 × 9 × 2 inches. Bake 10 minutes. Spoon marshmallow creme over hot layer. Let stand 1 minute; spread evenly. Drizzle topping over creme; sprinkle with 1 cup peanuts.

Bake until golden brown, about 20 minutes. Let stand until cool, then loosen edges from side of pan with wet knife. Cut into 3 × 1 1/2-inch bars with wet knife.

Serving Size: 1 Bar Calories 170 (Calories from Fat 70); Fat 8 g (Saturated 2 g); Cholesterol 10 mg; Sodium 125 mg; Carbohydrate 22 g; (Dietary Fiber 1 g); Protein 4 g

Chewy vs. Crunchy

Some people like their cookies crisp and golden brown, others like them chewy and just kissed with color. For chewy cookies, reduce the minimum bake time by one to two minutes, adjusting for your personal preference.

Strawberry-Chocolate Cheesecake Squares (p.85)

7

Bar Cookies and Brownies

Lemon Squares

25 squares

Go a little nutty! Add 1/2 cup flaked coconut into egg mixture for a chewy treat.

1 cup all-purpose flour
1/2 cup (1 stick) margarine or butter, softened
1/4 cup powdered sugar
1 cup granulated sugar
2 teaspoons grated lemon peel, if desired
2 tablespoons lemon juice
1/2 teaspoon baking powder
1/4 teaspoon salt
2 eggs

Heat oven to 350°. Mix flour, margarine and powdered sugar. Press in ungreased square pan, 8 × 8 × 2 or 9 × 9 × 2 inches, building up 1/2-inch edges. Bake 20 minutes. Beat remaining ingredients about 3 minutes or until light and fluffy. Pour over hot crust.

Bake about 25 minutes or until no indentation remains when touched lightly in center; cool. Sprinkle with powdered sugar, if desired. Cut into 1 1/2-inch squares.

Serving Size: 1 Square Calories 90 (Calories from Fat 35); Fat 4 g (Saturated 1 g); Cholesterol 15 mg; Sodium 80 mg; Carbohydrate 13 g; (Dietary Fiber 0 g); Protein 1 g

Date Bars

36 bars

To cut up pitted dates, use a sharp knife or kitchen shears. Rinse knife or shears in cold water when the blade becomes sticky.

Date Filling (below)
1 cup packed brown sugar
1 cup (2 sticks) margarine or butter, softened
1 3/4 cups all-purpose or whole wheat flour
1/2 teaspoon salt
1/2 teaspoon baking soda
1 1/2 cups quick-cooking oats

Prepare Date Filling; cool. Heat oven to 400°. Grease rectangular pan, 13 × 9 × 2 inches. Mix brown sugar and margarine. Mix in remaining ingredients until crumbly. Press half the crumb mixture evenly in bottom of pan. Spread with Date Filling. Top with remaining crumb mixture, pressing lightly.

Bake 25 to 30 minutes or until light brown; cool slightly. Cut into 2 × 1 1/2-inch bars.

DATE FILLING

3 cups cut-up pitted dates (1 pound)
1/4 cup sugar
1 1/2 cups water

Cook all ingredients over low heat 10 minutes, stirring constantly, until thickened.

Serving Size: 1 Bar Calories 145 (Calories from Fat 45); Fat 5 g (Saturated 1 g); Cholesterol 0 mg; Sodium 110 mg; Carbohydrate 25 g; (Dietary Fiber 1 g); Protein 1 g

Fudgy Oatmeal Bars

70 bars

2 cups packed brown sugar
1 cup (2 sticks) margarine or butter, softened
1 teaspoon vanilla
2 eggs
2 1/2 cups all-purpose flour
1 teaspoon baking soda
1/2 teaspoon salt
3 cups quick-cooking or regular oats
2 tablespoons margarine or butter
1 can (14 ounces) sweetened condensed milk
2 cups (12 ounces) semisweet chocolate chips
1 cup chopped nuts
1 teaspoon vanilla
1/2 teaspoon salt

Heat oven to 350°. Mix brown sugar, 1 cup margarine, 1 teaspoon vanilla and the eggs. Stir in flour, baking soda and 1/2 teaspoon salt; stir in oats. Reserve one-third of the oat mixture. Press remaining oat mixture in greased jelly roll pan, 15 1/2 × 10 1/2 × 1 inch.

Heat 2 tablespoons margarine, the milk and chocolate chips over low heat, stirring constantly, until chocolate is melted; remove from heat. Stir in nuts, 1 teaspoon vanilla and 1/2 teaspoon salt. Spread over oat mixture in pan. Drop reserved oat mixture by rounded teaspoonfuls onto chocolate mixture.

Bake until golden brown, 25 to 30 minutes. Cut into bars, about 2 × 1 inch, while warm.

Serving Size: 1 Bar Calories 130 (Calories from Fat 55); Fat 6 g (Saturated 2 g); Cholesterol 10 mg; Sodium 95 mg; Carbohydrate 18 g; (Dietary Fiber 1 g); Protein 2 g

Backpacker Bars

2 dozen bars

Need a quick energy boost? Grab one of these wholesome bars.

- 3/4 cup granulated sugar
- 3/4 cup packed brown sugar
- 3/4 cup (1 1/2 sticks) margarine or butter, softened
- 1 teaspoon vanilla
- 2 eggs
- 1 1/2 cups all-purpose flour
- 1 1/2 cups Golden Grahams cereal, crushed
- 3/4 cup quick-cooking or regular oats
- 1 teaspoon baking soda
- 1/2 teaspoon baking powder
- 1/2 teaspoon salt
- 3/4 cup chopped peanuts
- 1 cup (6 ounces) semisweet chocolate chips
- 1/4 cup chopped peanuts
- 2 tablespoons quick-cooking or regular oats

Heat oven to 350°. Mix sugars, margarine, vanilla and eggs in large bowl. Stir in flour, cereal, 3/4 cup oats, the baking soda, baking powder and salt. Stir in 3/4 cup peanuts and 2/3 cup of the chocolate chips.

Spread in ungreased rectangular pan, 13 × 9 × 2 inches. Sprinkle with 1/4 cup peanuts, remaining chocolate chips and 2 tablespoons oats. Bake 25 to 30 minutes or until golden brown; cool completely. Cut into about 2 1/4 × 1 1/2-inch bars.

Serving Size: 1 Bar Calories 225 (Calories from Fat 100); Fat 11 g (Saturated 3 g); Cholesterol 20 mg; Sodium 210 mg; Carbohydrate 29 g; (Dietary Fiber 1 g); Protein 4 g

Almond-Cherry Strips

About 4 dozen strips

For a little holiday magic, use both red and green candied cherries.

- 2 1/2 cups all-purpose flour
- 1 cup sugar
- 1/2 cup whipping cream
- 1/4 cup (1/2 stick) margarine or butter, softened
- 1 egg, separated
- 2 teaspoons baking powder
- 1 teaspoon almond extract
- 1/2 teaspoon salt
- 1 3/4 cups powdered sugar
- 1/2 teaspoon almond extract
- 1/4 cup chopped almonds
- 1/4 cup cut-up red candied cherries

Mix flour, sugar, whipping cream, margarine, egg yolk, baking powder, 1 teaspoon almond extract and the salt. Work with hands until blended. Cover and refrigerate at least 1 hour.

Heat oven to 375°. Divide dough into halves. Roll each half into rectangle, 8 × 6 inches, on well-floured, cloth-covered board. Square off rounded corners. Place on greased cookie sheet.

Beat egg white until foamy. Beat in powdered sugar gradually; continue beating until stiff and glossy. Do not underbeat. Beat in 1/2 teaspoon almond extract. Spread egg white over dough; arrange almonds and cherries on top. Cut into strips, about 2 × 1 inch. Bake until edges are light brown, about 10 minutes.

Serving Size: 1 Strip Calories 80 (Calories from Fat 20); Fat 2 g (Saturated 1 g); Cholesterol 5 mg; Sodium 60 mg; Carbohydrate 15 g; (Dietary Fiber 0 g); Protein 1 g

Banana-Sour Cream Bars

72 bars

1 1/2 cups sugar
1 cup dairy sour cream
1/2 cup (1 stick) margarine or butter, softened
2 eggs
1 1/2 cups mashed bananas (about 3 large)
2 teaspoons vanilla
2 cups all-purpose flour
1 teaspoon salt
1 teaspoon baking soda
1/2 cup chopped nuts
Vanilla Frosting (below)

Heat oven to 375°. Mix sugar, sour cream, margarine and eggs in large mixer bowl on low speed, scraping bowl occasionally, 1 minute. Beat in bananas and vanilla on low speed 30 seconds. Beat in flour, salt and baking soda on medium speed, scraping bowl occasionally, 1 minute. Stir in nuts. Spread in greased and floured jelly roll pan, 15 1/2 × 10 1/2 × 1 inch. Bake until light brown, 20 to 25 minutes; cool. Frost with Vanilla Frosting. Cut into bars, 2 × 1 inch.

Vanilla Frosting

2 cups powdered sugar
1/4 cup (1/2 stick) margarine or butter, softened
1 1/2 teaspoons vanilla
2 tablespoons hot water

Mix powdered sugar, margarine, vanilla and hot water. Stir in 1 to 2 teaspoons additional hot water until smooth and of desired consistency.

Serving Size: 1 Bar Calories 80 (Calories from Fat 25); Fat 3 g (Saturated 1 g); Cholesterol 10 mg; Sodium 75 mg; Carbohydrate 12 g; (Dietary Fiber 0 g); Protein 1 g

Peanut Butter Squares

48 squares

These chocolate and peanut butter squares are perfect with a big glass of milk!

1/2 cup granulated sugar
1/2 cup packed brown sugar
1/2 cup (1 stick) margarine or butter, softened
1/3 cup crunchy peanut butter
1 egg
1 cup all-purpose flour
1 cup oats
1/2 teaspoon baking soda
1/4 teaspoon salt
Peanut Butter Frosting (below)
3 tablespoons cocoa
1 tablespoon milk

Heat oven to 350°. Mix sugars, margarine, peanut butter and egg. Stir in flour, oats, baking soda and salt. Spread in greased rectangular pan, 13 × 9 × 2 inches. Bake until golden brown, 17 to 22 minutes; cool.

Prepare Peanut Butter Frosting; reserve 1/3 cup. Stir cocoa and milk into remaining frosting until smooth. If necessary, stir in additional milk until of spreading consistency. Frost with cocoa frosting. Drop Peanut Butter Frosting by teaspoonfuls onto cocoa frosting; swirl for marbled effect. Cut into about 1 1/2-inch squares.

Peanut Butter Frosting

1 1/2 cups powdered sugar
1/4 cup crunchy peanut butter
2 tablespoons milk

Mix all ingredients. Stir in additional milk 1/2 teaspoon at a time, until of spreading consistency.

Serving Size: 1 Square Calories 90 (Calories from Fat 35); Fat 4 g (Saturated 1 g); Cholesterol 5 mg; Sodium 65 mg; Carbohydrate 12 g; (Dietary Fiber 0 g); Protein 1 g

Strawberry-Chocolate Cheesecake Squares

48 squares

2/3 cup margarine or butter, softened

1/2 cup sugar

2 egg yolks

2 cups all-purpose flour

1 cup (6 ounces) miniature semisweet chocolate chips

2 packages (8 ounces each) cream cheese, softened

3/4 cup sugar

2 teaspoons vanilla

2 eggs

1/2 cup (3 ounces) miniature semisweet chocolate chips, finely chopped

1 cup strawberry jam

1/4 cup miniature semisweet chocolate chips

1 teaspoon shortening

Heat oven to 375°. Grease rectangular pan, 13 × 9 × 2 inches. Mix margarine, 1/2 cup sugar and the egg yolks in medium bowl. Stir in flour. Press evenly in pan. Bake 18 to 20 minutes or until golden. Immediately sprinkle with 1 cup chocolate chips. Let stand about 5 minutes or until chips are softened; carefully spread over baked layer. Refrigerate about 30 minutes or until chocolate is firm.

Beat cream cheese in medium bowl until smooth. Beat in 3/4 cup sugar, the vanilla and eggs. Stir in 1/2 cup chocolate chips. Pour over chocolate layer in pan. Bake about 30 minutes or until filling is set. Spread with jam. Melt 1/4 cup chocolate chips and the shortening. Drizzle over top of bars. Refrigerate about 3 hours or until chilled. Cut into 1 1/2-inch squares.

Serving Size: 1 Square Calories 150 (Calories from Fat 70); Fat 8 g (Saturated 4 g); Cholesterol 30 mg; Sodium 65 mg; Carbohydrate 18 g; (Dietary Fiber 1 g); Protein 2 g

Cream Cheese Squares

25 squares

1/3 cup margarine or butter, softened

1/2 cup packed brown sugar

1 cup all-purpose flour

1/2 cup chopped walnuts

1 package (8 ounces) cream cheese, softened

1/4 cup granulated sugar

1 tablespoon lemon juice

2 teaspoons milk

1/2 teaspoon vanilla

1 egg

Heat oven to 350°. Grease square pan, 8 × 8 × 2 inches. Beat margarine and brown sugar until fluffy. Mix in flour and walnuts until crumbly; reserve 1 cup. Press remaining crumbly mixture in pan. Bake 12 minutes. Mix cream cheese and granulated sugar; beat in remaining ingredients until smooth. Spread cream cheese mixture over crust; sprinkle with reserved crumbly mixture. Bake until center is firm, about 25 minutes. Cool; cut into about 1 1/2-inch squares. Store cookies in refrigerator.

Serving Size: 1 Square Calories 115 (Calories from Fat 65); Fat 7 g (Saturated 3 g); Cholesterol 20 mg; Sodium 60 mg; Carbohydrate 11 g; (Dietary Fiber 0 g); Protein 2 g

Perfect Squares

Line your pans with aluminum foil when making brownies (grease the foil if the recipe calls for a greased pan). The cooled brownies lift right out and are easily cut into uniform squares. Best of all, no pan to clean.

Chocolate Chip Bars

36 bars

1/2 cup granulated sugar

1/3 cup packed brown sugar

1/2 cup (1 stick) margarine or butter, softened

1 teaspoon vanilla

1 egg

1 1/4 cups all-purpose flour

1/2 teaspoon baking soda

1/2 teaspoon salt

1/2 cup chopped nuts

1 cup (6 ounces) semisweet chocolate chips

Heat oven to 375°. Grease and flour baking pan, 13 × 9 × 2 inches. Mix sugars, margarine and vanilla. Beat in egg. Stir in flour, baking soda and salt. Mix in nuts and chocolate chips. Spread dough in pan. Bake until light brown, 12 to 14 minutes. Cool; cut into bars, about 2 × 1 1/2 inches.

Serving Size: 1 Bar Calories 95 (Calories from Fat 45); Fat 5 g (Saturated 2 g); Cholesterol 5 mg; Sodium 80 mg; Carbohydrate 11 g; (Dietary Fiber 0 g); Protein 1 g

Toffee Bars

32 bars

1 cup (2 sticks) margarine or butter, softened

1 cup packed brown sugar

1 egg yolk

1 teaspoon vanilla

2 cups all-purpose flour

1/4 teaspoon salt

1 bar (4 ounces) milk chocolate candy, broken into pieces

1/2 cup chopped nuts

Heat oven to 350°. Mix margarine, brown sugar, egg yolk and vanilla in large bowl. Stir in flour and salt.

Press dough in ungreased rectangular pan, 13 × 9 × 2 inches. Bake 25 to 30 minutes or until very light brown. (Crust will be soft.) Immediately place milk chocolate pieces on baked layer. Let stand about 5 minutes or until soft; spread evenly. Sprinkle with nuts. Cool 30 minutes. Cut into bars while warm.

Serving Size: 1 Bar Calories 135 (Calories from Fat 70); Fat 8 g (Saturated 2 g); Cholesterol 5 mg; Sodium 90 mg; Carbohydrate 15 g; (Dietary Fiber 0 g); Protein 1 g

Linzer Torte Bars

48 bars

To cut the bars into triangles, first cut into squares and then cut each square diagonally in half.

1 cup all-purpose flour

1 cup powdered sugar

1 cup ground walnuts

1/2 cup (1 stick) margarine or butter, softened

1/2 teaspoon ground cinnamon

2/3 cup red raspberry preserves

Heat oven to 375°. Mix all ingredients except preserves until crumbly. Press 2/3 of mixture in ungreased square pan, 9 × 9 × 2 inches. Spread with preserves. Sprinkle with remaining crumbs. Press gently into preserves. Bake 20 to 25 minutes or until light golden brown. Cool completely.

APRICOT LINZER BARS: Substitute ground almonds for the ground walnuts and apricot preserves for the raspberry preserves.

Serving Size: 1 Bar Calories 60 (Calories from Fat 25); Fat 3 g (Saturated 1 g); Cholesterol 0 mg; Sodium 25 mg; Carbohydrate 8 g; (Dietary Fiber 0 g); Protein 1 g

Linzer Torte Bars

Pumpkin Spice Bars

49 bars

Dress up these bars for the holidays with candy corn or pumpkin candy decoration.

4 eggs
2 cups sugar
1 cup vegetable oil
1 can (16 ounces) pumpkin
2 cups all-purpose flour
2 teaspoons baking powder
2 teaspoons ground cinnamon
1 teaspoon baking soda
3/4 teaspoon salt
1/2 teaspoon ground ginger
1/4 teaspoon ground cloves
1/2 cup raisins
Cream Cheese Frosting (below)
1/2 cup chopped nuts

Heat oven to 350°. Grease jelly roll pan, 15 1/2 × 10 1/2 × 1 inch. Beat eggs, sugar, oil and pumpkin. Stir in flour, baking powder, cinnamon, baking soda, salt, ginger and cloves. Mix in raisins. Pour batter into pan. Bake until light brown, 25 to 30 minutes. Cool; frost with Cream Cheese Frosting. Sprinkle with nuts. Cut into bars, about 2 × 1 1/2 inches. Refrigerate any remaining bars.

CREAM CHEESE FROSTING

1 package (3 ounces) cream cheese, softened
1/4 cup plus 2 tablespoons margarine or butter, softened
1 teaspoon vanilla
2 cups powdered sugar

Mix cream cheese, margarine and vanilla. Gradually beat in powdered sugar until smooth and of spreading consistency.

Serving Size: 1 Bar Calories 150 (Calories from Fat 70); Fat 8 g (Saturated 2 g); Cholesterol 20 mg; Sodium 105 mg; Carbohydrate 19 g; (Dietary Fiber 0 g); Protein 1 g

Chewy Fruit-and-Walnut Bars

32 bars

1 cup packed brown sugar
1/2 cup (1 stick) margarine or butter, melted
1 teaspoon grated orange peel
1/4 cup orange juice or pineapple juice
1 teaspoon vanilla
2 eggs
2 cups all-purpose flour
2 teaspoons baking powder
1 package (6 ounces) diced dried fruits and raisins
3/4 cup chopped walnuts

Heat oven to 350°. Grease rectangular pan, 13 × 9 × 2 inches. Mix brown sugar, margarine, orange peel, orange juice, vanilla and eggs. Stir in flour and baking powder. Stir in dried fruits and walnuts. Spread batter in pan.

Bake 20 to 25 minutes or until wooden pick inserted in center comes out clean; cool. Sprinkle with powdered sugar, if desired. Cut into 2 × 1 1/2-inch bars.

Serving Size: 1 Bar Calories 115 (Calories from Fat 45); Fat 5 g (Saturated 1 g); Cholesterol 15 mg; Sodium 70 mg; Carbohydrate 17 g; (Dietary Fiber 1 g); Protein 2 g

The Ultimate Brownie

24 brownies

5 squares (1 ounce each) unsweetened chocolate
2/3 cup margarine or butter
1 3/4 cups sugar
2 teaspoons vanilla
3 eggs
1 cup all-purpose flour
1 cup chopped nuts
1 cup (6 ounces) semisweet chocolate chips, if desired

Heat oven to 350°. Grease square pan, 9 × 9 × 2 inches. Heat chocolate and margarine over low heat, stirring frequently, until melted; remove from heat. Cool slightly. Beat sugar, vanilla and eggs in large bowl on high speed 5 minutes. Beat in chocolate mixture on low speed. Beat in flour just until blended. Stir in nuts and chocolate chips.

Spread batter in pan. Bake 40 to 45 minutes or just until brownies begin to pull away from sides of pan. Cool completely. Spread with Chocolate Frosting (p. 59), if desired

Serving Size: 1 Brownie Calories 195 (Calories from Fat 110); Fat 12 g (Saturated 3 g); Cholesterol 25 mg; Sodium 70 mg; Carbohydrate 21 g; (Dietary Fiber 1 g); Protein 2 g

Marbled Brownies

36 brownies

Cream Cheese Filling (below)
1 cup (2 sticks) margarine or butter, softened
4 ounces unsweetened chocolate
2 cups sugar
4 eggs
2 teaspoons vanilla
1 1/2 cups all-purpose flour
1/2 teaspoon salt
1 cup coarsely chopped nuts

Heat oven to 350°. Prepare Cream Cheese Filling. Heat margarine and chocolate over low heat until melted; cool. Beat chocolate mixture, sugar, eggs and vanilla in large mixer bowl on medium speed, scraping bowl occasionally, about 1 minute. Beat in flour and salt on low speed, scraping bowl occasionally, about 30 seconds. Beat on medium speed about 1 minute. Stir in nuts.

Spread half the batter in greased baking pan, 9 × 9 × 2 inches. Spread with Cream Cheese Filling. Lightly spread remaining batter over Cream Cheese Filling. Gently swirl through batter with spoon in an over-and-under motion for marbled effect. Bake until wooden pick inserted in center comes out clean, 55 to 65 minutes; cool. Cut into bars, 2 × 1 inch.

CREAM CHEESE FILLING

1 package (8 ounces) cream cheese, softened
1/4 cup sugar
1 teaspoon ground cinnamon
1 egg
1 1/2 teaspoons vanilla

Beat all ingredients in small mixer bowl, scraping bowl occasionally, about 2 minutes.

Serving Size: 1 Brownie Calories 185 (Calories from Fat 110); Fat 12 g (Saturated 4 g); Cholesterol 35 mg; Sodium 115 mg; Carbohydrate 18 g; (Dietary Fiber 1 g); Protein 2 g

Vanilla Brownies

32 brownies

Vanilla extract, glaze and creamy chips give these moist bars rich vanilla flavor.

    1 2/3 cups (10 ounces) vanilla milk chips
    1/2 cup (1 stick) margarine or butter
    1 1/4 cups all-purpose flour
    3/4 cup sugar
    1/2 cup chopped nuts
    1 teaspoon vanilla
    1/4 teaspoon salt
    3 eggs
    Vanilla Glaze (below)

Heat oven to 350°. Grease and flour rectangular pan, 13 × 9 × 2 inches. Heat vanilla chips and margarine in heavy 2-quart saucepan over low heat, stirring frequently, just until melted. (Mixture may appear curdled.) Remove from heat; cool. Stir in remaining ingredients except Vanilla Glaze.

Spread batter in pan. Bake 30 to 35 minutes or until toothpick inserted in center comes out clean. Cool completely. Prepare Vanilla Glaze and spread on brownies.

Vanilla Glaze

    1 1/2 cups powdered sugar
    3 tablespoons margarine or butter, softened
    1 to 2 tablespoons milk
    1/2 teaspoon vanilla

Mix all ingredients until smooth.

Serving Size: 1 Brownie Calories 160 (Calories from Fat 70); Fat 8 g (Saturated 3 g); Cholesterol 20 mg; Sodium 75 mg; Carbohydrate 20 g; (Dietary Fiber 0 g); Protein 2 g

Turtle Brownies

16 brownies

This is the one for those who like cake-like, tender brownies.

    1 cup sugar
    1/2 cup shortening
    1 teaspoon vanilla
    2 eggs
    2/3 cup all-purpose flour
    1/2 cup cocoa
    1/2 teaspoon baking powder
    1/4 teaspoon salt
    1/2 cup coarsely chopped pecans
    12 vanilla caramels
    1 tablespoon milk

Heat oven to 350°. Grease square pan, 9 × 9 × 2 inches. Mix sugar, shortening, vanilla and eggs in large bowl. Stir in flour, cocoa, baking powder and salt.

Spread batter in pan. Sprinkle 1/2 cup coarsely chopped pecans over batter before baking. Bake 20 to 25 minutes or until wooden pick inserted in center comes out clean. Remove from oven.

Heat 12 vanilla caramels and 1 tablespoon milk over low heat, stirring frequently, until caramels are melted. Drizzle over warm brownies. Cool completely.

Serving Size: 1 Brownie Calories 170 (Calories from Fat 70); Fat 8 g (Saturated 2 g); Cholesterol 25 mg; Sodium 70 mg; Carbohydrate 23 g; (Dietary Fiber 1 g); Protein 2 g

Turtle Brownies

Butterscotch Brownies

16 brownies

1/4 cup shortening
1 cup packed brown sugar
1 teaspoon vanilla
1 egg
3/4 cup all-purpose flour
1/2 cup chopped walnuts
1 teaspoon baking powder
1/4 teaspoon salt

Heat oven to 350°. Grease square pan, 8 × 8 × 2 inches. Heat shortening in 1 1/2-quart saucepan over low heat until melted; remove from heat. Mix in brown sugar, vanilla and egg. Stir in remaining ingredients. Spread in pan. Bake 25 minutes. Cut into 2-inch squares while warm.

Serving Size: 1 Brownie Calories 135 (Calories from Fat 55); Fat 6 g (Saturated 1 g); Cholesterol 15 mg; Sodium 75 mg; Carbohydrate 19 g; (Dietary Fiber 0 g); Protein 1 g

Almond Brownies

36 brownies

2/3 cup shortening
4 ounces unsweetened chocolate
2 cups sugar
1 1/4 cups all-purpose flour
1 cup chopped almonds
1 cup chopped almond paste
1 teaspoon baking powder
1 teaspoon salt
4 eggs

Heat oven to 350°. Heat shortening and chocolate in 3-quart saucepan over low heat until melted; remove from heat. Stir in remaining ingredients. Spread in greased rectangular pan, 13 × 9 × 2 inches.

Bake until brownies begin to pull away from sides of pan, about 30 minutes. Do not overbake. Cool slightly. Cut into bars, about 2 × 1 1/2 inches.

Serving Size: 1 Brownie Calories 180 (Calories from Fat 90); Fat 10 g (Saturated 2 g); Cholesterol 25 mg; Sodium 80 mg; Carbohydrate 20 g; (Dietary Fiber 1 g); Protein 3 g

Mint Brownies

About 4 dozen brownies

When you're pressed for time, these brownies can be made in a snap. Try topping these minty brownies with wedges of chocolate-covered peppermint patties or shaved chocolate mint wafers for a "homemade" touch

1 box (1lb. 5oz.) Supreme brownie mix with pouch of dark chocolate flavor syrup.
1/4 cup water
1/4 cup vegetable oil
1 egg
20 to 24 chocolate-covered peppermint patties
Mint Fluff Frosting (below)

Heat oven to 350°. Grease bottom only of rectangular pan, 13 × 9 × 2 inches. Mix brownie mix (dry), Chocolate Flavor Syrup, water, oil and egg with spoon about 50 strokes or just until mix is moistened. (Do not use electric mixer.) Spread in pan. Bake 30 minutes.

Immediately after baking, place patties on brownies. Return to oven 3 to 4 minutes or until patties are softened. Spread evenly over brownies; cool. Frost with Mint Fluff Frosting. Cut into 1 1/2-inch squares. Refrigerate any remaining brownies.

MINT FLUFF FROSTING

1 cup whipping cream
2 tablespoons powdered sugar
1/4 to 1/2 teaspoon peppermint extract
10 drops green food color

Beat all ingredients in chilled bowl until stiff.

Serving Size: 1 Brownie Calories 130 (Calories from Fat 45); Fat 5 g (Saturated 2 g); Cholesterol 10 mg; Sodium 60 mg; Carbohydrate 20 g; (Dietary Fiber 0 g); Protein 1 g

Metric Conversion Guide

Volume

U.S. Units	Canadian Metric	Australian Metric
1/4 teaspoon	1 mL	1 ml
1/2 teaspoon	2 mL	2 ml
1 teaspoon	5 mL	5 ml
1 tablespoon	15 mL	20 ml
1/4 cup	50 mL	60 ml
1/3 cup	75 mL	80 ml
1/2 cup	125 mL	125 ml
2/3 cup	150 mL	170 ml
3/4 cup	175 mL	190 ml
1 cup	250 mL	250 ml
1 quart	1 liter	1 liter
1 1/2 quarts	1.5 liters	1.5 liters
2 quarts	2 liters	2 liters
2 1/2 quarts	2.5 liters	2.5 liters
3 quarts	3 liters	3 liters
4 quarts	4 liters	4 liters

Measurements

Inches	Centimeters
1	2.5
2	5.0
3	7.5
4	10.0
5	12.5
6	15.0
7	17.5
8	20.5
9	23.0
10	25.5
11	28.0
12	30.5
13	33.0
14	35.5
15	38.0

Weight

U.S. Units	Canadian Metric	Australian Metric
1 ounce	30 grams	30 grams
2 ounces	55 grams	60 grams
3 ounces	85 grams	90 grams
4 ounces (1/4 pound)	115 grams	125 grams
8 ounces (1/2 pound)	225 grams	225 grams
16 ounces (1 pound)	455 grams	500 grams
1 pound	455 grams	1/2 kilogram

Temperatures

Fahrenheit	Celsius
32°	0°
212°	100°
250°	120°
275°	140°
300°	150°
325°	160°
350°	180°
375°	190°
400°	200°
425°	220°
450°	230°
475°	240°
500°	260°

Note: The recipes in this cookbook have not been developed or tested using metric measures. When converting recipes to metric, some variations in quality may be noted.

Index

Page numbers in *italics* indicate photographs